RENEWING THE CONGREGATION

RENEWING
THE CONGREGATION

edited by

ROBERT W. LONG

AUGSBURG PUBLISHING HOUSE

Minneapolis   Minnesota

RENEWING THE CONGREGATION
Copyright © 1966 Augsburg Publishing House
All rights reserved
Library of Congress Catalog Card No. 66-22567

Scripture quotations are from the Revised Standard Version of
the Bible, copyright 1946 and 1952 by the Division of Christian
Education of the National Council of Churches.

Contents

III. Congregations in Mission

Foreword

The two decades after World War II have witnessed more sweeping changes in man's knowledge and control of his environment than any comparable period in history. In the twenty years since 1945 we have slowly come to realize that many of the old familiar landmarks are going or have gone. In an age where the computer, cloverleaf, jet plane, and space capsule are familiar symbols, our generation is bewildered and stunned by the staggering problems confronting it.

Leaders of business, education, government, and industry are confronted with radically changing situations and are discovering the excitement of exploring this new age and rising to the chance it presents for imaginative action.

Church leadership can do no less. The history of the church shows that its most vigorous activity comes in times of upheaval and change. There can be a resharpening of spiritual perception and a heightened sense of Christian adventure if we are ready to respond to the challenge of the times.

In a recent Gallup Poll the question was asked, "Do you think religion as a whole is increasing its influence on American life or losing its influence?" In 1957 only 14 percent of those who replied thought it was losing influence, but today that figure has risen to 45 percent. It is quite obvious that there are rising doubts in the minds of Americans concerning the influence and effectiveness of the religious establishment in the nation. We are told that on college campuses it is the organized church and not religion which is under fire.

The congregation is accused by many today of being irrelevant in the new age of science and secularism. Its critics argue that the present congregational structure developed in a society where the village and countryside were the typical setting for human activity and that it is unsuitable for mass urban society. In a mobile, urbanized society decision-making usually takes place in a variety of communities which are far removed from the place of residence. The residential parish is therefore considered incapable of exerting significant influence in the public realm. Too often, it is declared, congregational autonomy is so interpreted that no meaningful ecumenical or cooperative ministry can be developed at the grass roots. Others point out that the structure of the congregation has so involved the laity in building up the institution that there is no time or interest for carrying on God's ministry in the structures of society.

These charges and many others, which are often valid, have created a significant ferment in the church of today. "Is the local church out of date?" asks the *National Observer*. Then, in an attempt to throw light on the debate, it points to the fact that "the residential church has the human and financial resources to revitalize Christianity in America 1965. It accumulated them during the so-called 'religious revival' of the 1940s and 1950s, when church membership climbed from 49 percent to 64 percent of the population, and church construction increased almost tenfold to more than one billion dollars a year."

Faithfulness in our day demands that we be open to the guidance of the Holy Spirit and obedient to the leading of the Lord of the church. We will need to be realistic and sensitive to the new age in which we live, and the new dimension for mission which it demands. It is never possible to return to the first century or even to the first part of the twentieth. But no matter what the century or the setting may be, the church has been entrusted with the proclamation and witness of the Gospel in word and deed. Its structures must be tested in each new age in the crucible of God's mission in the world which he created and redeemed through the life and death of his Son.

It is not our purpose to defend some of the structures which have taken on the aura of tradition in many congregations, but rather to give our best thought to the renewal and enrichment of the congregation for its mission in this day. This is not the time for the church to cling nostalgically to shapes and traditions which are no longer useful for its witness in the new age. Neither is this the time to discard viable structures which are still capable of meaningful witness today. All Christian congregations in the United States could still be potential mission stations by the power of the Holy Spirit and the reshaping of their structures.

The contents of this book are the product of a conference on "The Role of the Congregation in the Mission of the Church" sponsored by the Division of American Missions of the National Lutheran Council. It was the purpose of the conference to provide new insights and stimuli for effective congregational mission. Attention was focused on congregation renewal, recognizing the vast potential for mission that is available now, and realizing that our mobile, pluralistic, urban society is forever challenging the church to experiment with new shapes and forms for its witness in the world.

ROBERT W. LONG

I.

The Mission of the Congregation

1.

David S. Schuller

The Purpose
of the Church

The pressures which demand a reexamination of the role of the congregation in the light of the church's purpose and mission are increasing. Many churchmen—pastors and laymen alike —are asking whether the residential parish has become an antiquated form. They are concerned that it has become simply another "place" among the established places and domains in the world—but one that is no longer on the mainstream of life. The institutionalized forms have come in for a major share of criticism.

And most demanding of all is the question regarding the extent to which we must look for God's presence today outside of the church. Can we point to lives that are changed apart from the church and the Gospel as evidence of God's activity in our world? Is such a view faithful to the Holy Scriptures, or does its rejection represent a narrow, foreshortened view of God's concern and activity?

How are we to formulate our answer? To what extent is the biblical material regarding the church prescriptive for our day? Are we dealing with descriptive material which gives us a glimpse of the form of church life as it first fashioned itself in Asia Minor, or is it prescribing norms and patterns that still are binding today? In view of the polemical background of our confessional writings, can they provide useful insights and models for fashioning contemporary ministries? Furthermore, how shall

3

we utilize the wealth of historical studies describing the church
as it sought to carry out its tasks amid a variety of cultural
backgrounds? What weight shall we give to the sociological
studies of the church which have begun to come into their own
within the last decade? Finally we are confronted with serious
descriptions which attempt to forecast the mode of life that is
emerging in the future. It is relatively easy to select one of these
disciplines or viewpoints and use it exclusively as a means for
defining the purpose of the church. No one discipline, however,
defines the total reality of the church. A contemporary man has
trouble recognizing the empirical church when he reads a
theological treatment of the church. A modern churchman has
trouble recognizing the church in its vertical dimension when
he reads a current sociological analysis.

In formulating our answer, we shall attempt to utilize primarily the biblical material as the source of our knowledge of
the church's purpose. Contemporary sociological and theological

———————◆———————

The discussion raised a theological issue which remained unre-
solved. Debate returned again and again to the relationship between
God's action in and through the church and everything God is doing
in the world apparently independently of the Christian community.
Can a distinction be drawn between God's providential action and
God's redeeming action? If the restoration and reconciliation of human
life is being achieved by the action of God through secular agencies,
what is the place and significance of faith? If the church is to be
wholly involved in the world, and its history, what is the true nature
of its separateness? We were able to state thesis and antithesis in this
debate, but we could not see our way through to the truth we feel
lies beyond this dialectic. Yet we believe that all attempts to adapt
the structures of the thinking of the church to match the great
changes that are taking place in the world will be doomed to paralysis
until we can find the way through to a truer understanding of the
relation between the world and the church in the purpose of God.

"The Witness of the Congregation in Its Neighborhood."
Section III, Final Report (World Council of Churches. Commission on World Mission and Evangelism, Mexico City, 1963),
p. 2.

questions will provide a means for evaluating the forms which these purposes have assumed today. An awareness of the future will enable us to begin to shape our policies so that we may be faithful in the emerging future.

As we proceed it will be necessary to void twin heresies in speaking about the church. They are, as Stählin has said, the same two dangers that arise in Christian thinking about Jesus Christ. The first pitfall is that of Docetism, wherein Christians had difficulty in thinking of Christ as being fully human. They could not take his manhood seriously and consequently spoke of him as though God had "clothed himself in appearance in the unreal mantle of human existence." Similarly most popular talk about the church is docetic. The true church becomes an invisible reality that exists only as an ideal in this world.

The opposite heresy was that of Arianism, in which the deity of Jesus Christ was taken in full seriousness. In reference to the church, such a spirit sees it as the whole noble outcropping of the human spirit, an indication of the essential restlessness and search of the soul for its fulfillment in its Creator. The church is cherished and prized, but it is no longer the place where God himself dwells with men; any sense of holiness, mystery, and "otherness" is gone. The divine mystery is reduced to that which the human mind can grasp and formulate.

———◆———

The church itself is regarded as the be-all and end-all of the Christian life. Indeed, some would even declare the church to be the final repository of the Kingdom of God, the ultimate product of God's entire creative activity. But the Christian community across the earth is becoming restless under the restraint of this obviously all too narrow vision of the purpose of God and of the role of the church in that purpose. The Christian people cannot rest easy with the specter of a lost world when the Gospel proclaims that God has come in Christ to save it. Nor can they rest easy with their self-image as the assured elect when their Master's life took the form of a servant, and He called them to the "way of the cross."

Arnold B. Come, *Agents of Reconciliation* (Philadelphia: The Westminster Press, 1960), p. 19.

The Church Is of God

Before we speak of the church's purpose we must remind ourselves briefly of the theocentric quality of the church. For the purpose of the church is *God's* purpose for it. The term *ecclesia*, the key New Testament concept usually translated "church," refers to the "redeemed community." The reference may be to a group of God's people gathered in a specific place; here the term may be translated "congregation." Acts 8:1; 1 Cor. 1:2; 1 Cor. 11:16; Col. 4:16. The same term is used with equal freedom to describe the whole Christian community without any reference to place. Acts 9:31; 20:28; Col. 1:24. In some passages it is difficult to determine which sense is intended. Gal. 1:13; 1 Cor. 10:32; 1 Cor. 11:22.

A critical reaction to our use of the term *ecclesia* would suggest that our accent has been too strongly upon the separation aspect of the term over against sufficient stress upon the *klesis*, God's call. Renewed emphasis upon this central feature would correct any "withdrawal from the world" mentality by recognizing the call as denoting God's action in Jesus Christ of inviting and moving people back into a relationship with himself. The Epistle to the Ephesians is particularly rich in its development of this point (Cf. Chapter 1:18 and Chapter 4).

———————◆———————

The movement of reform in the sixteenth century gave a stimulus to the re-thinking of the whole question of the relation between the Church and the world. But the establishment of regionally limited provinces of a Protestant *corpus christianum* with national state-churches prevented the European Protestant churches from realizing the impossibility of preserving the christianized world of the Constantine era. Thus they continued to live and think with the habits of the old Christendom, until in recent times they were taken by surprise at the rapid development of so-called "secularism" . . . That the Christian Church is living in, sent to, and serving a non-Christian world, is, however, a New Testament truth which many European Christians still hesitate to accept without reservation.

Report of the Theological Commission on Worship (European Section) of the World Council of Churches Commission on Faith and Order, p. 3.

Biblical emphasis is upon the redeemed community even when the word "church" is not used. Highly significant is the material in 1 Peter. Although the Petrine approach parallels many Pauline accents, the term *ecclesia* is not used in the epistle. Yet the letter is a rich analysis of the nature of the church during the period of the dispersion: "an elect race, a royal priesthood, a holy nation, a people for God's own possession" (2:9). "You are now the people of God" (2:10). "Let yourselves be built, as living stones, into a spiritual temple" (2:5). The people of God are now to live as "aliens in a foreign land." He describes what should comprise the style of their lives, how they are to react to human institutions, to government, jobs, and marriage (2:11-3:18.

It is virtually impossible to investigate the purpose of the church without utilizing one other biblical picture, that of the Body of Christ. This term provides several insights: (1) The people of God are intimately related to Jesus Christ because of

---

Docetic thinking about the church: "What is called on earth 'Church' is then but a shell, in itself neutral and non-essential, which can drop off and be destroyed. The Church which we love and believe in is a totally invisible quantity, and every attempt to discover or construct it on earth is to be condemned as 'fanaticism' (Ger. 'Schwärmerei')."

Arian thinking about the church: "Here the Church gets acknowledgment, perhaps is revered, may be beloved as well, because in her the most sublime expression of the spirit of man, the finest blossoming of human culture, finds its expression and abode. . . . From here can be found words of very lofty acknowledgment of the Church, praise for the need of her and her significance in the collective system of culture, words affirming the indispensability of religious instruction in connection with education, and anything else of the same sort. But the Church is no longer mystery. . . . The Church is no more the place of the divine incursion and attack: no more the home of miracle by which man can have intercourse with the hosts of another world."

Wilhelm Stählin, *The Mystery of God.* Translated by R. B. Hoyle (St. Louis: Concordia Publishing House), English Edition, 1964, pp. 131-32.

his redemptive work (Eph. 1:22-23; Col. 1:18-22); (2) the Body is composed of individuals who are related to one another in unity through Jesus Christ (1 Cor. 12:12-14; 24-27); (3) members of the Body are to utilize the gifts God gives them for the edification of the other members (Eph. 4:12-16); (4) pastors, teachers, evangelists, and prophets are gifts of God, given to equip the church for its ministry (Eph. 4:12; 2 Cor. 4:1-5; Col. 1:24-27).

As we discuss the purpose of the church, it will be useful to seek once again the intention of the creeds in describing the *nature* of the church as *una, sancta, catholica,* and *apostolica.* Further, in the Lutheran confessions the term "church" is defined as the assembly of believers. The classic formulations center in the Augsburg Confession (Articles VII and VIII and in the Smalcald Articles (Part III, Art. 12).

Recently parts of the Lutheran church have been wrestling with these formulations to make sure that such identifying marks of the church do not become restricted to use as a type of yardstick by which to measure the orthodoxy or rectitude of churches. Such an interpretation would present an overly static view of the Gospel and the Sacraments that would fail to see them as the power of God through which he is at work in the midst of his church.

———◆———

This calling action of God, and therefore the situation of being called is "through Jesus Christ" (I Cor. 1:26-31). This phrase sums up the entire action of God in sending His Son into the world to redeem the erring and sinful human race by His own suffering and death (Col. 1:12-20), in raising Him from the dead (I Pet. 1:2-5), and in commissioning the Word of the Gospel, by which men are summoned to have a share in this redemptive work (Col. 1:21-29; II Cor. 5:18-21). The call, or *klesis,* which summons God's people to be the church, or the *ekklesia,* is therefore a continuing call, a summons that does not stop, an abiding "calling." The significance of the church and of membership in the church is, simply stated, to be the setting and agency by which God's call in Christ keeps coming to His people (Eph. 4:1-16).

Richard R. Caemmerer and Erwin L. Lueker, *Church and Ministry in Transition* (St. Louis: Concordia, 1964), p. 22.

The Church Responds to God

In describing the purpose of the church we shall utilize three major categories, describing its functions over against God, itself as church, and the world. Any classification contains both advantages and inherent weaknesses. An initial difficulty lies in the distinction between objectives or outcomes and the means which effect such changes. Thus the initial response to the question of the church's *purpose* by the average Lutheran pastor is likely to be "to preach the Gospel and administer the sacraments." In reality one is not describing goal or purpose, but enunciating a means for effecting still undefined goals. A statement of purpose should provide some indication of how the church ideally should expend its time and resources.

———◆———

In Article VII the church is defined as the assembly of believers, and the assembly of believers is again defined by what happens within it: the church "is the assembly of all believers, in which the Gospel is purely preached and the sacraments administered according to the Gospel."

Thus the church is constituted by the act of preaching the Gospel and administration of the sacraments, and hence by the Christ who acts today through the Gospel and the sacraments. The church exists not where the Bible, the confession, and the ministry are merely possessed in silence, but where the Gospel is preached and the sacraments administered on the foundation of the Scriptures and in consensus with the fathers and brethren, and thus where the voice of Christ is heard and where Christ gives himself. This delivers the concept of the church from a false ontology as well as from an actualism without continuity.

In Article VII of the Augsburg Confession the church is called *una sancta ecclesia,* "one holy Christian church." In its essential nature it is the one church because it is the holy Christian, or "holy catholic and apostolic," church (Nicene Creed). It is one and holy because the Holy Spirit is working in it. It is one and catholic because the one Christ, the Lord of heaven and earth, governs it. (In the Book of Concord "catholic" is translated "Christian.") It is one and apostolic because its immovable foundation is the ministry of the apostles.

Edmund Schlink, "The Breadth of the Church of the Augsburg Confession." *The Lutheran World Review,* Vol. I, No. 3 (Jan. 1949), pp. 4-5.

The first purpose of the church is *worship of God.* We view the whole of the world as having been created for the glory of God. To fulfill his human nature man is to respond to God in trust, love, and service, which is the essence of worship. Sin has destroyed this basic relationship with God. One consequence of his disobedience is the fact that man now offers worship to that which *is not God.* In the thought world of the Bible the denial of worship was unthinkable. During the period of the Old Testament, the problem was the worship of gods other than Yahweh. In the New Testament man often worshipped the creature rather than God, Paul declares in Romans 1 and 2. In our day the question has taken another turn. Man is not asking which god to worship; he is questioning the fundamental concept of worship. Whether this is but a variation of the problem confronted by Paul or a new situation altogether is a question we deal with in our day.

The victory of Jesus Christ has set man free — free to worship with praise, thanksgiving, and service. Even in his worship redeemed man remains *simul justus et peccator.* While Christian worship represents that total and true worship for which man originally was created, yet it is continually threatened by idolatry. Worship is ever in need of purging and reform. The victory of Jesus Christ is for the redemption of *all* men. In her worship the

---

When the Committee for Research on Church and Ministry of The Lutheran Church — Missouri Synod outlined the functions of the church, they asked whether the functions of the local church differed from those of the church in greater areas. In suggesting the objectives of the Christian congregation in a given locality, they outlined the following:

a) Sustained and increased faith of members
b) New members added to the Body of Christ
c) Exercise of the priesthood of believers in self-consecration, sacrifice and worship
d) Mutual service of members to one another in love and good works
e) A surrounding community experiencing the leavening influence of the Gospel

Workshop on Church and Ministry, July 1963, p. 18.

church needs to remember that salvation is offered to *all* men. Although worship will involve primarily those within the Body of Christ, worship should in no way isolate Christians from those who are yet apart from God.

The church's worship of God extends into three areas. The Christian worships the Creator:

1. by giving him thanks and praise for life, which he not only has given but also maintains by the manifold daily gifts of his love;

2. by praying and interceding in the midst of threats and needs in this world for the whole of mankind;

3. by offering his whole body and life in daily vocation and service to his fellow men.

> Report of the Theological Commission on Worship (European Section) of the World Council of Churches Commission on Faith and Order, page 15.

This suggests that man is free to use the entire world in his worship of God. This relates our worship theologically to the doctrine of creation and provides the means for serving mankind responsibly. Prayer, in turn, embraces the whole of creation. The individual Christian is to be brought to a point where he prays regarding each aspect of life to which he has become sensitive. The world of technology, art, science, politics — the horrors of the world as well as its joys — become the subject matter of Christian prayer.

Finally, this reminds us that worship is meaningful only when it remains in vital contact with life. People may faithfully "go through" the rituals of worship; but they worship only when they have emerged from the real world of flesh and blood, of machines and commerce, of family and babies, of laughter and tears. Worship and world are two spheres into which the Christian alternately must plunge. Worship sanctifies a man to live and serve as a total human being *in the world*.

The church is able to carry out its task of worship because of the presence and the empowering of the Holy Spirit. Through baptism one becomes a member of the Body of Christ; he is marked by the seal of the Spirit; the kingdom of God has come

unto him. By his baptism he is called to that common service
to which the church is commissioned. He is strengthened for
this service through the Word, the proclamation of the Gospel,
and through the celebration of the Eucharist.

Worship and mission must be neither divorced from one
another nor set in opposition to one another. Since the Gospel
lies at the heart of Christian worship in creating man's response,
God's purpose for his entire creation is present in the worship of
his people. Worship, therefore, refers both to cultus — adoration
and praise given in the structure of liturgy — and to ethical
obedience. The early church knew both expressions of worship.
We run the risk of grave distortion if we give priority or sanction
to one over against the other. The temptation lies in both directions. Some would restrict worship to a cultic observation. Others
who interpret worship to include every deed of love done to a
fellow-man run the risk of disengaging those deeds from the
gifts which God bestows through Word and Sacrament as these
are found in the cultus.

The Church Serves the People of God

The second task of the church is to *sustain and upbuild the
faith of its members.* The Gospel that Jesus proclaimed implied
fellowship among men. At the outset he called twelve men to be
with him. The heart of this calling of men into fellowship was

———◆———

There is the mission of the Church to the modern world. Christians are still in danger of suffering from an inferiority complex, owing
very largely to our habit of regarding Christianity as a way of religion
for the individual; about our personal piety we have naturally a certain
shyness. But Christianity is in the first place faith in the God to whom
the world belongs, and in Christ as the Savior of all mankind. Either
the Gospel which we have believed is not true, or it is a Gospel for
all mankind and no men can live their lives rightly without it.

A. G. Hebert, *Liturgy and Society: The Function of the Church
in the Modern World* (London: Faber and Faber, Ltd., 1935),
p. 14.

something more fundamental than a means of extending the proclamation of the kingdom or the beginning of an ecclesiastical order that would develop into an ecclesiastical structure. Jesus created a fellowship of disciples because the Gospel he proclaimed demanded it. He was the center of this fellowship. The disciples were bound to one another because they were bound to him.

The Gospel, then, determined the nature and the activities of the church in its youth. This is not to suggest that the early church was unaware of its surrounding culture or that it was not, to an extent, influenced by it. It argues, however, that the tasks and activities of the early church were not copies of the patterns of groups and organizations about them — either religious or secular. The patterns were distinctive because they were distinctive expressions of the Gospel. The Gospel did not become a conscious norm against which such activities were measured. Rather the Gospel was seen as a power which changed lives radically and thus effected new relationships.

Before speaking of the mission of the church in the world, then, we find it necessary to discuss the concern of the church with its internal edification. Rather than discuss whether the *being* of the church is necessarily prior to its *mission,* we simply observe the vital interrelationship. The two concerns are close; many structures of the church serve both tasks. But it is necessary to distinguish between the two. Where the church loses con-

———————◆———————

In order to guarantee the proclamation of the Gospel and to manifest his presence among his people, Jesus Christ has vouchsafed to his Church the preaching of the Word and the Sacraments of Holy Baptism and Holy Eucharist. The Church receives these gifts and obeys his commands when it "continues in the apostles' teaching and fellowship, in the breaking of bread and in prayers" (Acts 2:42). It is, however, the Spirit, and not the Church, who gives life to the means of grace ordained by Christ, so that the Church cannot presume to command and distribute their benefits, but must ask the Spirit to quicken them ever anew according to Christ's promise.

Commission on Faith and Order, *op. cit.*, p. 21.

sciousness of this distinction, she is likely to become either a self-satisfied group in-bent upon its own satisfactions with no sense of mission or an activistic group involved in every endeavor of good will but without the power that comes from God.

Through the mutual edification of its members the church as the Body of Christ strengthens itself against all of the forces in the world which would tear it down. "Edification" is the key Pauline term for this process. It becomes most clear if we think simultaneously of two biblical pictures of the church — the building whose stones hold one another in place and the body whose members need the service of the other members. In Ephesians 4 the concept of edification is yoked with another which has essentially the same thrust, namely, "speaking the truth in love."

The need for edification, for sustaining and increasing faith, highlights one aspect of the task of Christian education within the church. Our Lord sent his church to make disciples of all nations, teaching them to observe all that he had commanded. This involves instructing and guiding the youthful generation that is maturing within the church. Through their baptism they have been incorporated into the Body of Christ. An understanding of what discipleship involves comes through the patient instruction of the fellowship. Where this fails we experience the rejection of their faith and of the church when they become adults. It is during the early years of their lives that children and young people determine in their own minds how vital the church is in their world. When they are able to make their own decisions as adults, they will move away from the life of the

———————◆———————

On the one hand are the structures for maintaining the *being* of the church; on the other hand, the structures for fulfilling the *mission* of the church. So, logically, the structure for mission would seem to deserve first consideration. But experimentally, in the human perspective, being drawn into a community of people who know spiritual renewal in Christ comes first. And out of this experience arises naturally and inevitably the sense of mission.

Come, *op. cit.*, pp. 74-75

church if the church demonstrates that it is dealing only with peripheral matters in highly dogmatic fashion.

The task of education has just as much to do with the life of adults. The adult's edification of faith should not suggest that it somehow deals with a sphere of life apart from his daily world of activity. That is to say, his growth in faith must go hand in hand with his understanding of the meaning of the faith in all of the circumstances of his life. Thus the local church can become the cross-point at which some of the critical problems facing people are discussed in the light of the Christian faith. The Body of Christ grows in its understanding of God's will in changing circumstances as it studies the Holy Scriptures in common. Such discussions must be dialogical. They must confront the reality of the world as it is conveyed through the lives of its members. Discussions must be on an adult level, which means avoiding carefully predigested topics that are safely removed from any area of conflict.

The third task of the church is closely related: *mutual service.* The Gospel, we have said, brings man into a twofold relationship: with God and with other people. Within the fellowship we find worship and edification, and here we also find the channels for service. This service does not arise as obedience to lofty ideals; it is the spontaneous reaction of the new life of faith and love to situations in need of it. When a man trusts in God, the inevitable corollary is love and care for his fellow man. The

———◆———

. . . for work in his service, to the building up of the Body of Christ. So shall we all at last attain to the unity inherent in our faith and our knowledge of the Son of God — to mature manhood, measured by nothing less than the full stature of Christ. We are no longer to be children, tossed by the waves and whirled about by every fresh gust of teaching, dupes of crafty rogues and their deceitful schemes. No, let us speak the truth in love; so shall we fully grow up into Christ. He is the head, and on him the whole body depends. Bonded and knit together by every constituent joint, the whole frame goes through the due activity of each part, and builds itself up in love (Eph. 4:12-16 NEB).

church reflects the concern of the Shepherd who seeks the one straying sheep; it becomes the Good Samaritan who is more concerned with the wounded than with itself. It remembers the insistence of her Lord, of Paul, Peter, and James that the Christian must be a doer as well as a bearer of the Word.

God provides the gifts the church needs for this service. The Body of Christ, Paul makes clear, is not a homogeneous mass of duplicate members. Each is given specific gifts; there is a rich diversity of gifts to provide for a diversity of service. These diverse gifts and ministries are perhaps seen most clearly when the three major lists in Ephesians, 1 Corinthians, and Romans are compared in parallel columns:

Eph. 4:11	*1 Cor. 12:28*	*Rom. 12:6-8*
apostles	apostles	
prophets	prophets	prophecy
evangelists		
pastors		
teachers	teachers	teaching
	workers of miracles	service
	healers	exhortation
	helpers	contributing
	administrators	aid
	speakers in tongues	acts of mercy

———◆———

The common good, to which each member contributes by fulfilling his unique capacity, is the building up of the Body of Christ, the church. By these ministries the church is built up both quantitatively and qualitatively. Quantitatively the membership is increased and spread by *proclamation (kerygma)* of the Word of God (Jesus Christ) in such a way that men are led to encounter God, to hear His call and claim on their lives, and so are brought to decision. Qualitatively the membership of the church is intensified in its faith by the *teaching (didache)* of the Word to those who became Christ's disciples, "until *we all* attain to the unity of the faith and of the knowledge of the Son of God, to mature manhood, to the measure of the stature of the fullness of Christ" (Eph. 4:13).

Come, *op. cit.*, p. 84

The ministry of the church for the edification and service of the Body of Christ is as rich, then, as the composite list arising from these columns. Although Paul does not make the point explicit, he suggests that this broad ministry of service will include every member of the church. Over against a tendency to focus upon a small spiritual elite, the emphasis here broadens to include every gift God has given to his church. No one can reject the service of another since every form of ministry is necessary "for the common good" (1 Cor. 12:7; 12:26). Further, there is no prestige connected with exercising the gift since it comes from Christ. It is to be used as by a servant. "Whoever would be great among you must be your servant" (Matt. 20:26; Phil. 2:7-8).

Two significant changes have taken place in the church's understanding of its diaconic task. First, the work of service has moved from a position of an admirable "extra" task of the church to where it is evaluated as a symptom of a church's vitality. As the disparity between the affluence of the organizational church and given disadvantaged segments of the population became

---◆---

The purpose of all our schemes for the education of the young in the church is their incorporation into the life of the church. The single greatest cause of the church's failure in the training of its young — and the reason why so many who have been at Sunday School and in the youth organizations are rarely seen afterward in church — is that there is *no full, demanding, and attractive life into which to be incorporated* . . . . If children can see — and this is manifestly true in many cases — that what they are learning in church does explain how their parents and the other people they know in church live, and the choices and decisions they make, then this teaching becomes relevant and indeed exciting . . . rather are they aware that the choices and decisions of their parents and of the adults of the church are made on other grounds than those of Christian love and service. It is the contradiction between what they are taught in church and school, and adult life as they see it, that makes the gap between youth and the church.

Mark Gibbs and T. R. Morton, *God's Frozen People* (Philadelphia: The Westminster Press, 1964), pp. 118-19.

more pronounced, the church was forced to reexamine its own heart. The organized church began to repent of its flight from such people in need and "rediscovered the inner city." A half generation of angry young clerics began to work with these people in their need. Angered by the religious enterprise that had neglected such blatant need, they began to serve. For them diaconic service could never again become an "extra" for those of special interests. Secondly, diaconic work has moved increasingly from being the province of special interest groups within the church to being the task of the *whole* church. As one exploratory study phrased it, this marks the transition of *diakonia* from an "option" of a society to an "office" of the church.

The Church's Responsibility for the World

The fourth purpose of the church involves its *outreach into the world* to win others to the Body of Christ. Because of its belief in the action of God in Jesus Christ in saving the world, the church finds that it must witness to this good news. A church which fails to truly hold to God's action as the crucial center of

---◆---

We must not overlook, therefore, the importance of such activities [works of love and care] in the life of the New Testament Church. Where this work of caring receives its proper place, the gospel is really understood and accepted. Where this work of caring is displaced or ignored for the sake of ecclesiastical politics or questions of order and authority in the organization of the Church, then the gospel is not being experienced. So we must not take for granted the humanitarian impulse of the New Testament Church. We must not attribute this to a naive and unformed Christianity which as it grew more mature would pay more attention to the theological formulation of the faith and the ecclesiastical organization of the fellowship. . . . [these] have at times been allowed undue prominence so that the fundamental truth of the gospel has been overlooked that caring for one's fellow men is an essential of the gospel, that just as worship is the expression of our relationship to God, so deeds of caring are an expression of our relationship with our fellow men.

L. G. Champion, *The Church and the New Testament* (London: The Carey Kingsgate Press Ltd.), pp. 109-110.

all history will not be able to sustain a missionary effort with the patience and endurance that such a witness demands. "We cannot but speak of what we have seen and heard" (Acts 4:20) becomes a statement of faith and of fact by the church sustained by the Gospel. Witness is a clear and compelling obligation upon every Christian, congregation, and the whole of the Body of Christ. One who has experienced the liberating power of God is claimed by God to declare his wonderful deeds to other men.

In responding to the missionary task, the church bears witness in action to its own profound belief in the universality of the Gospel. Historically it has been so easy verbally to profess Christ as the Savior of the whole world, but still acting in such a way that he in fact became restricted to certain groups of people and became the giver of values to certain civilizations and cultures. The fact that the Word of God is not bound means proclaiming the Gospel to peoples of alien cultures so that they may respond to it in forms that may be quite different from those known by the sending church. An apostolic church fears imposing a "culturally conditioned brand of Christianity" upon other peoples.

The church appears again to be entering a period of testing because of its missionary character. Within our century it has been demonstrated again that as long as the church keeps the

————————◆————————

In this section we shall draw upon the papers and reports of the World Council of Churches' Commission on World Mission and Evangelism which met in Mexico City in 1963. The final report on "The Witness of Christians to Men of Other Faiths" comments on the motive for witness:

"These great themes [creation, covenant, reconciliation and witness] all reveal the purposes of God towards his total creation, together with the joyous response which the Holy Spirit evokes from man. In all of creation God has given to man in particular the capacity of responding to love. It is man to whom God has bound himself in covenant relation. His purpose is no less than the reconciliation of an alienated world to himself in Christ. The Christian, therefore, must be bold to appeal to all men to respond to what has been done for them and to claim all things for Christ. The Christian mission is the proclamation of this message to the whole world: Be ye reconciled to God" (p. 1).

faith to herself, trouble is avoided. Conflict begins when the church insists upon proclaiming that God "commands mankind, all men everywhere, to repent" (Acts 17:30). Many were martyred during the days of Hitler in Germany, not because they were Christians, but because they insisted on proclaiming the lordship of Christ over all of life. The period from the middle of the 19th century to the middle of the 20th century, when missions were an accepted part of modern civilization and thus received general encouragement from the world, has come to an end. The church is under pressure in many areas of the world. The number of people who live outside the reach of any organized evangelistic and missionary thrust has vastly increased. Many non-Christian religions have adopted the missionary methods of Christian churches and have entered many lands that have been traditionally Christian. The right of the church to carry on mission work is being challenged in an increasing number of countries.

Our world is changing faster than ever before. New patterns of life are taking shape. In our own country personal and community life is undergoing profound changes. The single residential neighborhood has given way to various systems of "neighbors" with whom a man interacts in residence, work, politics,

---

Visser 't Hooft described five major opponents of a missionary church in today's world: The *totalitarian ideologists,* those who pretend they want a clean ideological fight with the church for the minds, particularly of young people; in reality they use strong administrative pressures to restrict the work of the church. Secondly, there are the *syncretists,* those who are calling for an integration of all of the high religions of the world into an all-inclusive religion. Thirdly, there are the *internationalists;* concerned with the peaceful coexistence of the countries of the world, they fear Christian missions as a form of cultural invasion. Next there are the *cultural nationalists,* who see religion as part of one's cultural heritage which is to be defended. Finally there are the advocates of universal tolerance, often people of great heart and mind, who consider the missionary spirit as a spirit of arrogance.

"Missions as the Test of Faith," p. 4.

recreation, training, and worship. The variety of these plus the fact of ever-increasing mobility offers significant new dimensions to the task of Christian witness. For the church the change has demanded the creation of new forms to meet emerging needs. It is the task of mission that has made the question of forms so vital.

Congregations are seeking ways to utilize the institutional forms already at hand to meet the new demands for witness. Renewal has taken several significant shapes: (1) Cell groups are being formed in the new communities of people, in residential communities, in areas of industry, business, and commerce, and on various levels of political and civic life. Their goal is to bring the Word to bear upon those areas of life where important decisions are made affecting the lives of many. (2) Congregations are attempting to break the bonds that in the past have limited the group in terms of class, income, race, occupational level of responsibility, culture, and concern. (3) The church through its total membership is being utilized to bring its witness into the "streams of contemporary life where the fabric of human existence is being woven." The laity is seeking training that will equip them for their task as they move about in this nation or in other countries in government, and in industrial or educational positions. "The church is to equip its people to be God's servants in the world, and new forms of congregational life are needed for the fulfillment of this calling."*

Finally, the church has a *prophetic task of interpreting the events of its day in the light of God's revelation.* This involves speaking God's total message of judgment and grace upon every situation in life. Because Jesus Christ is Lord of all creation, no sphere of life can claim autonomy. All of history and all of life — even among those who reject his claim of lordship — is ultimately under his control. Each age has had its unique frontiers which our Lord has bade his church to cross. In our day he sends us out into the secular world.

---

*"Witness of the Congregation in Its Neighborhood." WCC—CWME, Section III, Final Report, p. 3.

Over against earlier generations we realize that a simple negative judgment upon the "secular world" is inadequate. We are more likely to see secularization as a neutral process that opens possibilities of both new freedoms and new enslavement for men. Part of the process of secularization involves increased control over nature by science and technology. This is but the latest expression of man's dominion over nature, which is part of God's intended purpose. These techniques open the possibilities of providing mankind with more adequate food, clothing, shelter, health, and leisure than ever before in history. However, secularization also has meant that man has greater difficulty in seeing the hand of God in daily life and therefore finds himself losing his sense of meaning and purpose in life. A form of secularization has infected the church itself as it has tacitly agreed that "religion" is simply another category of life that is restricted in influence.

A church conscious of its prophetic task over against society will not restrict its efforts to the remedial work of social welfare, but will become involved with the preventive aspects of this task by working with social education and action. Thus Christian social responsibility manifests itself in two directions: (1) In social welfare work directed toward the immediate physical and temporal needs of the individual; and (2) through social action

---◆---

Secularization appears as the revolutionary attempt of man to become emancipated from all forms of dependency. It is occurring in different forms and at different speeds in various countries of the world. In this dynamic situation the destiny of men is in the balance between greater freedom and new enslavement. Will he choose the emancipation which is in accord with the teaching of the Old Testament prophets and of Jesus in the Sermon at Nazareth, or the rebellion against his Maker which can only destroy his life? As Christians we are involved with all mankind in the process of secularization and with the making of these choices which present themselves not once but again and again.

"Christian Witness to Men in the Secular World." WCC—DWMW. Section II (Mexico City), pp. 2-3.

that addresses itself to the underlying conditions that produce the need for welfare work. Over against the distribution of Christmas baskets to the needy, the responsible Christian is more concerned with the fundamental questions of justice and working conditions which cause such cases of poverty in the first place.

Effective witness in this area — as in the missionary task and its service — demands corporate action. The problems we face in any community, state, or nation are of such magnitude that unilateral action is hardly responsible. This does not imply disloyalty to one's confessional standards. But it does involve an openness directed to the other person and toward another denomination. We seek unity at every point possible. Our Lord

———————◆———————

16. The pattern of Christian mission in the secular world must therefore be one of constant encounter with the real needs of our age. Its form must be that of dialogue using contemporary language and modes of thought, learning from the scientific and sociological categories, and meeting people in their own situations.

17. The Christian message to man in the secular world is not only the proclamation of a transcendent God Who reigns as the Lord of nature, but also the proclamation of God as the Lord of world history, who became man in Christ. His divinity has become visible in His true humanity, as He emptied Himself to be one of us so that men might fulfill the tasks to which they were ordained in creation.

18. The Christian message to man in a secular world is not only to be expressed in terms of a religious inwardness which calls men out of this world. It must be expressed in terms of relations here and now, as restoration of man's total relationships, as the making whole of the person in Christ, the new man, who reconciles men in one and the same act to each other and to God. He is the gracious God in being our gracious neighbor.

19. The Christian message to men is not concerned with individuals but with the Kingdom of God as the destiny of mankind only as a whole. The Christian message liberates us for service to our neighbors. Being released from a selfish life, we can use the gifts of God which He has given to us in the process of secularization so that we do not victimize ourselves and others. Technical skills, scientific knowledge, the time of leisure, and the power structures receive their meaning in the service of others.

"Christian Witness to Men in the Secular World," p. 4.

is one; his Gospel is one. In many parts of the world and within our own culture, as churches we face essentially the same challenges, suffer because of the same problems, and attempt to render the same obedient response. Common planning and joint action must be instituted in every area where such action is feasible.

Conclusion

Whenever the church has faced the challenge of meeting situations in changing cultures, of moving into new lands, or of expanding her work into another frontier of culture, she has been forced to reexamine her own fundamental purpose in the world. To do this she has returned to her source in the Holy Scriptures and to her understanding of the Bible as developed in her creeds and other confessional statements. At the same time the church has learned to listen in an effort to understand the contemporary world. In our exploration today we have suggested that the church's primary purpose can be set into three fundamental relationships that involve five primary tasks:

I. The church responds to God in her worship.

II. The church serves the people of God in sustaining and up-building the faith of its members and in mutual service.

III. The church manifests her responsibility for the world in evangelistic outreach and in the prophetic task of proclaiming God's judgment and grace upon all of life.

2.

Nils A. Dahl

The Essential Nature of the Congregation

The Problem and Its Actuality

Does the New Testament presuppose or prescribe some ordering of the congregation, in a form that should be regarded as a binding norm for church life in the present age, as in all ages? This question has been actualized by a number of experiences, made by the churches in the last decades.

Ecumenical encounters have made churches all over the world realize that patterns of congregational life may be very different from the forms which are familiar to us from our own churches. Various traditions and structures have been confronted with one another: European and American, Lutheran and Anglican, Protestant and Catholic, Western and Eastern, old churches and younger churches, established churches and free churches, have met. These encounters have given new urgency to old questions: What is essential for the being of the church? What belongs to its well-being? What is necessary? What is good? What is permissible? What is biblical? What kind of ordering is appropriate for the future?

The struggle of the German church during the Nazi period, and the struggle of other European churches during the years of German occupation, made it clear to many that the ordering of the church and the structure of the congregations are not theological adiaphora. The Gospel can be denied not only

25

through false doctrines but also through actions which are contrary to the Gospel, and, possibly, by "heretical structures." The application of the "Arian Paragraph," by which persons of Jewish birth were excluded from the church and its ministry, was a clear, unambiguous case. Segregation and "Apartheid" in the congregation are other examples of a similar type. Paul's way of handling the conflict concerning table fellowship in Antioch (Gal. 2:11 ff.) is a clear biblical paradigm.

Missionary experiences, in America and Europe, as well as in Asia and Africa, have made the inherited structures of parish life appear to be questionable. To a large extent these patterns would seem to correspond to the social structure of rural communities. Perhaps the ordering of our congregations is outdated in a period of industrialization, urbanization, and rapid social change? Is the conservative institutionalism of many churches a hindrance to the spreading of the Gospel? Do the congregations function as centers to which outsiders are drawn, as was the case in the early church and its missionary expansion? Speaking out of my European background, I might even ask: Where do we find a congregation to which one can, without hesitation, bring a man who is interested and open to the Gospel? Is it not too often the case that there is, in fact, room only for persons of some special social class or psychological type? The Gospel cannot be brought to modern man simply by means of translating it into a language and a terminology that he can understand. Often, I suspect, the alienation of men from the church is due to sociological rather than to intellectual reasons. The social structure of our congregations may perhaps be one reason for the fact that many do not think the Gospel to be credible. Those who are not able to feel at home in a congregation cannot easily learn to understand the language of the church. The consequence of all of this might be that the historically given and incrusted structures are appropriate neither to the times nor to the matter. In this respect, I assume, the situation is much the same in secularized, Western countries and in areas where small, Christian minorities are living in non-Christian environments.

These predicaments have caused a quest for new forms of evangelism and "missionary presence," as e.g. professional groups, neighborhood groups, industrial missions, campus ministries, special groups of action, Evangelical Academies, and others. I assume that also the "non-church movement" in Japan should be mentioned in this connection. The World Council of Churches has initiated a series of studies and consultations on the theme "The Structure of the Missionary Congregation." Here the questions have been sharpened. Is the inherited structure of parish congregations not just a relic from the age in which ecclesiastical and secular orders were knit together within a "corpus christianum"? Does it not belong to the past, as does the whole period of post-Constantinian Christendom? Is it not, today, necessary to make a fresh start, beginning with structures of a new type which would serve the mission of God, rather than conserve patterns of the past? One possible form would be "little congregations" (witness and service groups, ad hoc congregations, cells, and so on), for which the "house churches" of New Testament times are supposed to provide the prototype.

Over against such tendencies a number of counter-questions have been raised, within the framework of the ecumenical study program as well as outside of it. Is everything dynamic and flexible? Is there no normative ordering with regard to the structures of the congregation? Isn't there, after all, something which should stand firm and not be subject to change according to variation of what happens to be the present situation? Even in this perspective the question becomes acute whether or not the Bible contains a norm or, at least, some guidance. Which, if any, elements of New Testament church order have a permanent, normative significance?

Hermeneutical and Methodological Considerations

The question with which we are dealing was laid before me originally by a group of ministers and theologians within the Lutheran churches of Scandinavia. My task has been to try to give an answer, and to do so as an interpreter of the New

Testament. But evidently the questions cannot be answered by simple reference to exegetical and historical matters of fact. The questions raise hermeneutical problems. The use of historical and critical methods in biblical scholarship has provided new possibilities for objective argumentation in questions of denominational and confessional controversies. Historical research is not able to give answers when the question is raised: What is normative? It is quite possible to agree in the description of the data and yet differ in the theological interpretation. Historical insight has made us aware of the variety and complexity of the data and thus in some respects made the problems more difficult than ever.

As far as we can see, a uniform order of congregational life never existed within the primitive church. Structure and forms of organization were, it would seem, not the same in Jerusalem, Antioch, Ephesus, Corinth, and Rome. Charismatic and institutionalized ministries, presbyterial and episcopal orders may exist simultaneously, or they may be combined in one way or another.

The New Testament does not contain any uniform doctrine of the church. Paul, Matthew, Luke, John, and the rest of the New Testament writers, all speak about the church and its ordering in their own way, with a terminology and a total conception of their own. Readership and situation, individuality and presuppositions of the writers vary. How is it possible to find out where the norm is to be found and how it is to be defined?

In the New Testament we find not only a variety of theologies, but also a succession of epochs within the earliest history of Christianity. A complex development, with many trends and many layers, led from the ministry of Jesus in Galilee and Jerusalem to the first apostles and the Jewish-Christian congregations inside and outside Palestine, thence to Gentile Christianity and, through Paul, or outside of his sphere of influence, to the early Catholic church of the second century. Many points remain obscure but, nevertheless, it is possible to reach a considerable agreement concerning the factual course of history. But thereby only little is gained for the evaluation of the development. Are we to find the authentic norm in the words and the attitude of Jesus himself, in the earliest congregation, in Pauline and Johannine theology, or in those scriptures which contain the last word of the Bible to questions of church order, the Pastorals and 2 Peter? Is the norm to be sought at the origin or in the result of the development which is reflected in the New Testament, or should the organic process of evolution or, perhaps, the flexibility as such be considered to be normative? Historical observations and inferences are not able to provide an answer to the question for a norm. Where some would like to trace the guidance of the Holy Spirit, others are inclined to ascertain a number of deviations or even an apostasy from the first love, or from the authentic understanding of Christian existence.

The completion of the canon of the New Testament did not bring history to stagnation. Centuries lie between us and the New Testament congregations. Structures of society and patterns of thought have changed. Even if we wished, we would not be able to restore New Testament forms of congregational life. Attempts of repristination always lead to results which differ from the models which one intends to revive. Church history is there, and we are not able to delete it. Any application of biblical norms to the present life of the congregation, in fact even the way in which the question of biblical norms is stated, is interdependent on church history and the evaluation of it. The hermeneutical problem cannot be isolated from the problem of Scripture and tradition, a question which in our days has been re-actualized for all churches and denominations.

Having indicated some of the complexities of the hermeneutical problem I may, nevertheless, venture to suggest some methodological principles. Descriptive, historical, and exegetical presentations cannot offer definite answers to the questions of the essential nature of the congregation and of biblical norms for its ordering, but they do provide a presupposition for an appropriate discussion of these questions. Problems of the ministry and of baptism could serve as very illuminating examples in this respect. The exegete is not appointed to serve as an umpire in questions of ecclesiastic controversies. He can only act as an expert adviser. The historian has to ascertain that all ideas of the church and all forms of congregational life are conditioned by social and historical circumstances. New Testament ecclesiology is, mostly, not abstract but concrete. The writers do not set forth static, timeless definitions and ideal orderings of the church. They do, much more, make theological statements concerning the historically given church and congregations present at given times and places.

The difficulties are not to be solved by means of liberation from the historically given confessions in order to enter upon inter-church dialogues, in the hope that this would be the way to reach a common, ecumenical, and biblical theology. The attempts which till now have been made in this direction certainly have had their value. But it appears to be difficult to reach beyond generalities. From the rich variety in the Scriptures, a comprehensive, unified view of New Testament theology can be obtained only if you take your position at one specific point and, thus, have one perspective. You may interpret the New Testament from the point of view of an all-inclusive Christo-centricity, or of the history of salvation, or of existential interpretation, or of a "non-religious approach." There is always the danger that a normative significance will be attached to the point of view, whereas insufficient attention may be given to the actual, rich, and manifold content of the canonical Scriptures.

The church is the *"first fruits"* of the new creation, a representative part of the whole. This is truly a biblical idea, and it is a fruitful term for looking at the church and its mission. But in the New Testament it is one image among many. In the ecumenical studies on the missionary structure of the congregation, the conclusion has sometimes been drawn that the church is simply ahead of the world and does not stand in opposition to it. It speaks to the world, not from above, and not in opposition, but from ahead. Here consequences are drawn which in this form are not biblical. An opposition of the church to the world is quite simply there in the New Testament whether we like it or not.

The idea, in some statements at least, seems to be that the

church is ahead of the world because the church already knows what the world still has to be told, namely, that the whole world is already redeemed and stands under the lordship of Christ. In the documents about congregational structure which are known to me, nothing is said about the last day and the separation brought by the last judgment. At this point there is a remarkable contrast to the ecumenical studies which in the years 1956-59 dealt with "The Lordship of Christ over the World and the Church."

It is very questionable whether any essential progress could be made by exchanging one "biblic-theological" point of view for another. Such a procedure could result in just another ecumenical type of theology in addition to the already existing confessional types. The historical concretion, the situational relativity, and the dialogical character of New Testament directives have to be taken seriously. It is impossible to regard every directive as equally and simultaneously normative. The demand for flexibility of structures and for courage to imperfect orderings is quite legitimate. In the New Testament there are warnings both against legalistic traditionalism and against enthusiastic disorder. The church is constantly facing a double danger, to conform to the world and to retire from the world. No exegesis, no biblical theology, and no dogmatics is capable of formulating norms which could release us from the risk of making our own decisions.

Rather than attempt to obtain a comprehensive theological view I would propose a much more modest procedure. The questions: What is the nature of the congregation, and, What are the biblical norms for its ordering, can only receive answers of general and fundamental validity if they are put in a very simple way. We have to ask: What constitutes the existence of the congregation as *ekklesia tou theou,* church of God. The basic concern must be to find out what is necessary and what is sufficient. Granting all possibilities of variation, what has to be there if a congregation is to be a right congregation? What would be the consequences for the normal structures and functions of a congregation? I would therefore propose that the question of New Testament norms for congregation ordering should be put in the form of the question of the marks of the church.

When I start with the old question of the *notae ecclesiae,* the marks of the church, this does not mean that my concern is the conservation of inherited forms. To the contrary, I am convinced that we have to differentiate strictly between inherited structures and permanent marks of the Christian congregation.

This method should lead to an assertion concerning the essential nature of the congregation with neither of the terms "essential" or "nature" being subject to any strict definition. What can be achieved will be a kind of minimal standard which would allow for a wide scale of variation with regard to practical orderings and theological interpretations. It should, however, be perfectly clear that this kind of presentation cannot exhaust the normative significance of New Testament orderings and injunctions. Attention should be given to the whole of Scripture in its full plenitude and rich variability, but it should really be the Scriptures which are allowed to speak, without having to pass through the filter of some systematized biblical theology or standard dogmatics. When biblical guidance is sought for congregational life in the present, everything depends on our capacity to discern what is the appropriate word and the pertinent analogy for the given situation. To this purpose that wisdom is needed which is a gift of the Holy Spirit. General considerations cannot reach beyond some basic elements.

Marks of the Church and Structures of the Congregation

The *Gospel* has been preached and has to be preached. Through the preaching of the Gospel the foundation has been laid for every single congregation as for the whole church universal (1 Cor. 3:10 f.; 11:1 ff.). The Gospel is the message of Jesus Christ, his coming, his death, and his resurrection. As a report of what has happened, once and for all, it is at the same time an offer of salvation and a call to faith. It is the proclamation of God's fulfillment of his promises, entrusted to the apostles as authorized messengers (Rom. 1:1-6; 1 Cor. 15:1-11; cf. Luke 24:44-49; Acts 2:22-29; 10:33-43; 13:23-39).

The Gospel message is for the *world.* Christ died for all, he is made Lord of the universe, and is to judge the quick and the dead. Until his coming in glory Christ exercises his lordship on earth through the preaching of the Gospel. Witness is borne to him before the tribunal of the world. Thus the existence of the church, and of all congregations, is based upon the mission of God, who sent his Son, his Spirit, and his messengers.

The Gospel is a proclamation of Christ, not of the church. But wherever the Gospel is heard, the church is created. Men are called together, congregations come into being. This, by necessity, implies a separation between men who acknowledge God and believe his Word, and those who reject it. As head of the universe, Christ has been given to the church, which is his body (Eph. 1:22 f.; Col. 1:18; 2:10). Thus the church is made distinct from a world which is secluded in itself, although the lines of frontiers may not be clearly visible to us. This distinction is perverted wherever it makes the church seclude itself from the world in self-sufficiency. Through the fact and the way of their existence the congregations should make God's universal will of salvation known to the world and its powers. The church has to be distinct from the world — in order to be church for all men.

The Gospel message includes the invitation to *baptism* and the *promise of the Holy Spirit.* What gives meaning and substance to baptism is not so much the external act of a symbolic bath as it is the name of Jesus and all that this name implies. The confession made by the person who is baptized, or on his behalf, as response to the question of faith is a constitutive element of the act of baptism. The baptismal event has to be appropriated and retained through faith in the triune God.

Baptism marks the transition from a past "once," without Christ, to the "now" and "forever" with Christ. It is not merely an announcement of a reality which would be present even without baptism. Something has happened to the person who was baptized—however, this should best be formulated in a doctrine of the sacrament of baptism. The baptized ones have to be taught, so that they may remember that they have been baptized into Jesus Christ and understand all that this fact does imply (cf.

e.g. Rom. 6:1 ff.; 1 Cor. 6:1-11; 12:13 ff.; Col. 1:12 f.; Hebr. 10:19 ff.; 1 Peter 1:22 ff.). The social structures of the congregation have to be tested as to whether or not they do promote a common life of those who are baptized into the name of Jesus, in conformity with the calling of God.

The community of those who are baptized is *gathered in the name of Jesus* for worship, with preaching, thanksgivings, and prayers.

Christ died for all; in the congregation he is adored and confessed as the One who died for us. The members of the church are reminded of what it means to belong to Christ in his church, and they are urged to testify, through their entire way of life, to what Christ has done for them. Thus, there are differences between missionary preaching (the kerygma) and the congregational preaching which has confession of faith as its presupposition, although this distinction is not always a clear one.

The normal form of a congregation is that of a local church, a group of men and women who have the possibility of coming together as physical persons. According to New Testament standards it is certainly a scandal if divided groups exist in the same area, mutually recognizing one another as Christians, and yet are either not willing or not allowed to come together in church fellowship.

In the assembly of the whole congregation it should become visible that "there is neither Jew nor Greek, there is neither slave nor free, there is not male and female" (Gal. 3:28). That does not mean that natural and social differences disappear, but that in the congregation men and women find each other, as different and yet one in Christ. In the name of Jesus persons come together who differ according to sex, age, race, ethnic background, vocation, and interest. No one should feel excluded or be considered inferior because he does, or does not, belong to any one particular group. In the same way, no one should be excluded because he lacks some special spiritual gift or some definite type of religious experience (cf. 1 Cor. 12).

For good reasons it has been questioned whether our geographically delimited parish congregations are, today, still valid expressions of the local unity of the Christian congregation. If the parish is delimited according to some social stratification rather than according to residence, the question becomes only more obtrusive. But special groups, made up of persons of the same vocation, age, concern, or other common characteristics, can never, in any legitimate way, replace the assembly of all those who call upon the name of our Lord Jesus in one place. What the "place" is at which people actually live today is a question that has to be answered by a sociologist rather than by an exegete. Most likely, we would have to give the term a very fluid definition so that the phrase "at one place" would cover both larger areas and units smaller than the limits of an average parish. The goal must be renewal of comprehensive local congregations. The nature of the congregation calls for inclusiveness; its functions cannot be taken over by other agencies for contacts between special groups.

The local congregation does not exist in isolation, but only in spiritual communion *(koinonia)* with all of those who call upon the name of Jesus, in every place. This spiritual communion even has to manifest itself in external ways (cf. e.g. 2 Cor. 8-9). For "house churches" and special groups it is especially important that they do not isolate themselves but stand solidly together with the whole church, in open exchange with other "little congregations."

The Lord's Supper is, in a symbolic form, the common meal of the congregation. Through prayers of thanksgiving *(eucharistia)* the memory of Jesus is celebrated, and the bread and the cup are his body and blood.

Holy Communion, like baptism, is not given either its right place or its full meaning if it is regarded as some isolable rite, a necessary or dispensable part of individual practice of piety. It is related to the whole event of redemption, not just to the specific act of institution in the last night of our Lord's earthly ministry. Its significance is due to what has happened, the death and resurrection of Jesus, and also to what is still in the future, the coming of Jesus and the perfect table fellowship in the kingdom of God. The celebration of the Lord's Supper is not only a testimony to but also a realization and an anticipation of the communion with Jesus.

According to New Testament understanding, the common, eucharistic thanksgiving constitutes table fellowship, regardless of whether the meal is an ordinary or just a symbolic one. By contrast, the later history of eucharistic practice may be characterized by slogans such as isolation, individualization, clericalization, doctrinalization, or spiritualization.

Common participation (koinonia) in the body and blood of the Lord creates fellowship (koinonia) among the members of the church (1 Cor. 10:16 f.). The gift implies a demand. An appropriate celebration of the Lord's Supper involves, according to the New Testament, much more than dogmatic and liturgic correctness. Those who are together at the table of the Lord should behave as brothers and sisters in their mutual relationships with one another (1 Cor. 10 and 11). As a token of reconciliation and love the kiss of peace, practiced by the first Christians at the Lord's Supper, is a symbol that indicates a norm, even though the rite may no longer be practiced.

To the celebration of the Lord's Supper as a symbolic, common meal of the whole congregation belongs the offering of gifts, as does also the service performed to those who lack what they need for their daily life, or who, due to sickness or age, are not able to attend the gathering of the congregation. Diaconical and economic stewardship is no peripheral aspect of a congregation's life, but is in an integral manner related to the right celebration of the Lord's Supper. Even though the practice of the first congregations cannot be imitated in an external way, it gives, even in this respect, lines of direction for the renewal of the congregation and its social structures.

In the congregation there must be *order*. The nature of the ordering is pneumatic, but it also has legal aspects. The power to bind and to loose (the power of the keys) is exercised through preaching and liturgy, mostly in conditional form (cf. 1 Cor. 11:27 ff.; 16:22; Gal. 1:8 f.; 1 John 1:6-10). In given circumstances it has to be given specific application with regard to individual persons or heretical doctrines (e.g. Matt. 18:15-20; 1 Cor. 5; 1 Tim. 1:20; 1 John 2:18-20). Both the institute of penance in Roman Catholicism and the "public discipline" practiced in ancient Protestantism led to misuses by which this type of church discipline was compromised and came into disrepute. In modern Protestantism it has become obsolete; what remains is hardly more than some relics. But the impasse should not veil the fact that the power of the keys is one mark of the New Testament congregations. The congregation must be in the position to be capable of saying "no" and not only "yes." Church discipline is not only motivated by care for erring individuals. The New Testament emphasizes just as much that the church should profess an unambiguous loyalty to Christ and be conserved as the holy temple of God (cf. e.g. 1 Cor. 3:17).

The apostles received a special commission as ambassadors of Christ and founders of the churches. A further delegation of this specific apostolic authority does not seem to have been anticipated. But the commission to preach has to be passed on, and new ministers of the Word have to be ordained, even though this may not necessitate any specific form of ordination. At the local level authority belonged, in apostolic times, to the congregation with its leaders. The *ekklesia* (church and/or congregation) was an assembly capable of decision. What was proposed, or in a preliminary way decided by the leaders, was accepted by acclamation of the gathered people (cf. Acts 15:22-28; 1 Cor. 5:3 f.). Legal forms may have varied, and cannot be taken as absolute norms. Yet the practice of the first congregations indicates some lines of direction for the present. It is contrary to the New Testament if the congregation is simply made a passive object of the preaching, liturgical, pastoral, and executive activity of the clergy. But it would not be any more biblical if the ministers were reduced to chosen functionaries of the congregation.

The Reformers' insistence upon the ministry of the divine Word as the one ministry in the church was legitimate as a protest against a hierarchical system. It leads, however, to disastrous consequences when the inference is drawn that the parish pastorate is the only type of office in a congregation. The Greek term *diakonia* means office, ministry, and service. According to Paul, each member of the congregation has his spiritual gift, his service, and his function (1 Cor. 12:4 ff.).

There is, in principle, no exclusive contrast between what is spiritual and what is legal. The idea of the New Testament writers is, rather, that the Spirit of God creates legal order in the church. According to its nature, church law is neither state law nor corporation law. What matters is not so much formal legality, with exact delineation of spheres of authority and competence, as it is the question of what conforms to God's jurisdiction. The standards are set by the Gospel, the confession of faith, and the Holy Spirit and are given to the church. Even an apostle has no right if he does not act in accordance with the truth of the Gospel (cf. Gal. 2:11 ff.). Special directives, which serve the purpose of good order, regulate the practice but do not constitute the essential nature of the congregation. A local congregation should not arbitrarily disregard the practices of the universal church (cf. 1 Cor. 11:16; 14:34-36). By giving his Spirit and his blessing, God may grant his approval of innovations which run contrary to established practices. Thus, Gentiles were recognized to be full members of the church, equal to the Jewish believers, because God had recognized them and poured the Holy Spirit out, even on them. The approval of church authorities was but an acknowledgment of this fact (Acts 10:44; 11:18; 15:7-11; cf. 2 Cor. 3:3; Gal. 2:1 ff.; 3:2-5; 4:4 f.). The structures of the congregation should not be fixed to a degree that might prevent the free action of the Holy Spirit.

Outlook

The congregation is called to be a missionary congregation The problem of its ordering should not be treated in isolation from its mission, but must be understood in relation to God's total design and action for the world. As the Creator of the universe, God is at work even outside the church, in severity and goodness. The church should calmly take notice of the ongoing secularization, the process of increasing social differentiation and desacralization. God loves the world, not the church alone. Christ is Lord of the whole world, not merely of the church or of a christianized world. The believers are in the world, not of the world, but sent into the world (John 17:11; 17:16, and 17:18). Thus, it is true that the congregation's essential nature is to exist for the sake of others. This does not mean that church and congregation are merely instruments of God's love for the world, or agencies for the work of Christ. The church is also a goal in itself (cf. e.g. John 17:19 and 17:22-26; Acts 20:28; Eph. 5:25 ff.; Tit. 2:14).

The mission of the church in the world has both centrifugal and centripetal aspects; persons are sent out, and men and women are drawn near. At the time of the ancient church the congregations seem in general to have grown by means of attraction; Paul's apostolic ministry is almost the only known example of a great "missionary enterprise." This may well be an indication of a norm; the congregation should be so shaped and structured that men are attracted by its very existence. Yet the way of God's dealing with the world is not completely circumscribed by terms such as centrifugal and centripetal. According to the Bible, God often acts in a way which could better be called "ec-centric" or "off center."* He finds instruments and shows his grace outside the realm which properly should have been in the center (Israel, Jerusalem, the church). This is not only often evident in the Old Testament; it is also an outstanding feature of the whole ministry of Jesus. God acts in a way that may be called "ab-normal," as it does not conform to the stated standards. In a different form, the same pattern reappears in Paul's interpretation of God's dealings with Israel and the Gentiles (Rom. 9–11). Thus, what is normative in New Testament congregation orderings should not be stressed in such a way that no room is left for what is "ab-

---

*In the ecumenical discussions on the missionary congregation, the term "eccentric" has been used in a way which differs from my usage. The world has been said to be the center, and the church to be off center. (Hoekendijk). I would, therefore, draw attention to the fact that my own terminology dates back to a W.C.C. consultation on the theology of missions, 1960.

normal" and "ec-centric." But it should not be overlooked that biblical statements of God's gracious dealing with Gentiles mostly are directed to God's own people, threatening doom and calling for repentance. In so far the congregation remains in the center of attention.

To maintain Gospel preaching, baptism, the local, comprehensive gathering, the Lord's Supper, and the "power of the keys," as marks of the church, determinative for the basic structure of the congregation, does not mean any churchly conservatism. The established structures of the present are to a very large extent determined by secondary historical and sociological factors. The marks of the church are still there, but mixed up with traditions of man which hinder the essential nature and the proper functions from being really determinants of the total structure of the congregation. The need for reformation and revival is not only evident because we live in an age of rapid social changes, but it is just as much a consequence of those factors which are constitutive for the existence of the congregation as such. Orderings which have become protective armors for ecclesiastical or congregational self-satisfaction and self-sufficiency have to be criticized with full biblical right. Seeking for new ways and orderings, one has to venture experiments, and not shrink back from what is unusual and perhaps even "abnormal." But in all of this it should not be overlooked that what a congregation owes to its environment is, next to the Gospel, first of all that it should be a right congregation, representative of the whole church of God. For instance, if the congregations in America had really been what they are destined to be as churches of Christ there would have been no racial antagonism within their own midst. For the world, politics, and society, this would likely have meant much more than special church declarations and actions aiming at a political solution of race problems.

In my considerations I have consciously limited myself to some basic aspects of a complex problem. This limitation might be a positive contribution, preventing overall summaries of biblical theology and quasi-philosophical analysis of the past history and the present situation to become more prominent in discussions on the proper ordering of the congregation than they ought to be. I will have achieved my goal if I have succeeded in making it clear that far-reaching consequences follow from those factors which are basic and constitutive to the congregation. At some points I have suggested what these consequences might be. An attempt to do more would surpass the competence of an exegete. But at this point there is certainly a need for further reflection.

3.

The Congregation

Theodore E. Matson   as a

Missionary Force

Representatives to a conference on the structure of the congregation agreed that congregations are "come structured," "care structured," "pastor structured," but not "go structured." The Central Committee of the World Council of Churches at a meeting in Rolle, Switzerland, affirmed that "the average congregation is apt to be an introverted community which does not think primarily of its obligation to bring the knowledge of Christ to its whole neighborhood and to the world." Congregations give the impression of being structured for everything except mission and evangelism.

Pierre Barton, a leading journalist of Canada, in an article titled "Out of This World," writes: "In the great issues of our time, it seems to me, the Christian Church as a whole has been a follower and not a leader. In issues as widely separated as capital punishment, birth control, nuclear armament, racial conflict, business ethics, sexual revolt, the Church has opted out; it has left the job of pioneering, of taking unpopular but farsighted stands, to the atheists, agnostics, unitarians, journalists, psychiatrists, sociologists, physicists, muckrakers, and politicians. The state of tension which should exist between the Church and society, the divine discontent, which is peculiarly Christian, has somehow been lost by an institution which has turned in upon itself, which has become so preoccupied with the status symbols, new edifices, the members' game of Sunday attendance, the comfortable pew atmosphere of the local parish, and above all the need to be saved in order to be successful."

Michael Barkway, editor and publisher of *Financial Times of Canada,* comments, "We run campaigns for 'church extension' and often find ourselves behaving like rival banks or oil companies, grabbing for the choicer corner sites in new districts and then trying to build a flossier plant than our competitors. We pretend that we are laboring in the vineyard to bring more nonbelievers into the family of God, but when we've got the new hall and church building, the kitchens and the organ — and the mortgage; when we've lured a congregation and collections start to roll in each week; is the kingdom of God really any nearer? Or have we merely the most flourishing club in the neighborhood?" A news commentator has said, "Most of our church activities are so petty and so tawdry that they seem completely irrelevant to the world where people are, working, living and dying. When the churches become primarily interested in their own property, and self-perpetuation, like any other business organization, they offend the good sense of mankind and insult the name of God."

We need to find a way of life in the church which both helps us to be better Christians and tells the pagan world something important about ourselves as in Christ. We must have a form of life which is organic to the nature of the church. This means some expression of life in the church which says that we are essentially a community joined together in Christ, and not just a collection of individuals who happen to have a taste for religion, or even a collection of congregations that carry on their ministries autonomously. We must find a way which will give full scope to the lay ministry and all the diversity of gifts of the laity. We need a way which emphasizes the importance of the home and the family, which gives room for sacrifice and love of a sacrificial nature, which makes the church the channel for the Gospel, a way in which the church can meet the world. This is a way of life that is struggling to be born in the church today.

Mission Begins at the Altar

The congregation can never be a missionary force unless it is open on the Godward side — a congregation that says, "Speak, Lord, for thy servant heareth." The congregation as a missionary force begins at the altar and returns to the altar. This means worship that senses afresh the presence of God. We must again put first what is often put last: namely, God, who is the object of worship and whose presence we celebrate. The First Commandment must come first, "I am the Lord thy God, thou shalt have no other gods before me." Too often we leave the house of God mindful of everything except the glory, the ceaseless love, and the majesty of God. It must be the glory of God that fills the temple, not the glory of the preacher, no matter how eloquent he is; and not the glory of the choir, no matter how angelic their anthems are; and not the glory of the worshiping congregation, no matter how sincere and devout they are. It is this living glory of God that the living church must jealously guard, lest God be dethroned in the very hallowed place consecrated to his worship. Only when this happens will the people of God come into his presence both with awe and with expectation.

The privilege of worship is ours because of God's self-giving to us, his self-revelation, his prevenient action. Without this, we never could have known that God is gracious, forgiving, and merciful. "For through him," writes Paul, "we both have access in one Spirit to the Father. So then you are no longer strangers and sojourners, but you are fellow citizens with the saints and members of the household of God, built upon the foundation of the apostles and prophets, Christ Jesus himself being the chief cornerstone, in whom the whole structure is joined together and grows into a holy temple in the Lord; in whom you also are built into it for a dwelling place of God in the Spirit" (Eph. 2:18 ff.). In worship, through Word and sacrament, God's people are drawn together to their Lord, and are cleansed, fed, renewed, and given strength for their tasks.

The question persists, how many of us come to church to be the Christian community brought together because Christ is present in Word and sacrament? We come to church as individuals to build up our soul muscles "as we would our bodies, with Wheaties." This sectarian sense of individual commerce with God without being living cells in and sharing in the Christian community — so foreign to Luther — seems to prevail among us. We make our common confessions, we sing together our common hymns of praise, we feed at the eucharistic banquet table, without any consciousness of taking part in a family affair and in the cementing of the family relationship. Are we the body of Christ, or just a collection of people who go to church? Are we the people of God, or merely an assortment of individual Christians? Are we the Christian community, or simply a group of like-minded people?

The worship of God precedes man's witness in the world. Worship first and mission second is a reflection of our Lord's summary of the law: first, "Love the Lord thy God," and then, "Love thy neighbor." First we say, "Hallowed be thy name." Then, and only then, do we say, "Thy kingdom come." Power and the know-how for the mission come from first having raised our hearts and minds to God. The mission is his, not ours. To inquire as to the relative importance of worship and evangelism is like asking the question, "Which is more important, eating or drinking?" The only possible reply to such an absurd question is to say that any man will sicken and die if he neglects either. In the presence of men in the world the church evangelizes, but in the presence of God the church worships.

We are so prone to fall into the heresy of thinking that worship and mission are something that we do. Rather, worship and mission are the sphere of our response and obedience to God's summons. Are we not stressing the importance of our response more than the grace of our summons? By the same token, we speak of worship and mission and service — which is all to the good, provided we know and acknowledge that it is not our service but his service. "I am among you as one that serves." Unless we gratefully accept his service to us, we cannot serve others. Until he has reconciled us, we cannot be the ministers of reconciliation.

It has well been said that "The church possesses the mysteries of Word and sacrament only as a steward; their ownership belongs only and solely to Christ. The Church will be judged not by the way in which it protects them or saves them, much less by the way it protects or saves itself by them, but by the way in which it uses and spends them so as to increase with the 'increase of God.'" God has humbled himself that we might be exalted as "laborers together" with him in his husbandry and in his building. It is this understanding that will remove the present "mission compound" mentality of the average congregation and what J. B. Phillips calls the "God in a box" religion. It is this world into which God comes, for which God cares, and in which the Word of God resides.

Each congregation must be the center for two interrelated activities: bringing people to worship God, and exercising people in Christian work. In other words, a congregation must be open to God and open to the community and the world. By this polarization, every activity of the church's program can fit in. The mission of the congregation is to be the body, the group joined together in Christ. It is the community, the cell, the team, which bears the responsibility for carrying on the mission. In the words of Bishop Robinson, "It is *God's* labor union."

The local congregation holds the key to a deeper, more meaningful understanding of the liturgy, which is the "work of the people of God." It is the acceptance of the responsibility for the mission of the church which ought to be the uniting factor among congregations. There must be the uniting of the two components, often out of touch with each other — worship and community, liturgy and society. In order to be the body of Christ, the church must look both toward heaven and toward men. A distinction here is most important. Whereas the mission is rooted in the special situation of the church militant in a fallen world, the necessity of worship is rooted in the eternal being of the whole church. In the kingdom of God every function of the church except that of worship will be taken from her. For the kingdom of God is the triumph of absolute love, and of that intercourse of God and man in worship which is love's most perfect work.

The Field Is the World

The congregation then becomes what it is intended to be — a channel for the Gospel. The program of the congregation becomes the connecting link between the altar and the community. If the local congregation is serving as an effective channel for the Gospel, its total life will reflect God's saving action, so that his love will actually touch the everyday life of each member and endow him with purpose, freedom, and power — and through each member touch the life of the total community. This will mean that their common worship, their common study, and their separate and joint activities will proclaim the Gospel, and they will keep asking why they do what they are doing. Then its program and structure will not permit members to let themselves down easily or let the congregation down easily in its relationship to other congregations and to the whole church. If the local congregation's program lets men down easily, the proclamation of the Gospel turns out to be meaningless words. It is within this framework of reference that we come to a dynamic understanding of the royal priesthood of believers. With this understanding of parish life, there is no ultimate difference between pastors and laymen — no first or second class church membership; instead, "a diversity of gifts but the same spirit working all in all." It is the common ministry of all members.

We must relate the two communities — the congregation and the parish — or we make nonsense of the Gospel. If we are alive to our responsibilities, the people of our community, starting with the person next door — no matter who he is — then we are more likely to see beyond next door to our responsibilities in Kenya, Tanzania, and Madagascar. The local congregation, whether it is in the heart of the city, in the suburb, or in the crossroad village, is the all-important cell in the total organism of the church, and the worship and the witness of the people are decisive. When all is said and done, the local congregation is a cell planted in a community by God himself to the end that the community might be affected by the church as dough is affected by yeast. The leaven must be in the lump.

How can the Christian and the congregation be isolated from the life of the community? Do not polities and work impinge upon the most private matters? Do not peace and war, racial crises, urbanization, cybernetics, poverty, juvenile delinquency, medicare, affect the daily existence of ordinary people? Is it not when and where the churches are the most estranged from and the least involved in the common life of the world that the churches are the most worldly?

If the congregation is the servant of her servant Christ, can she shun anyone? Did he shun the adulterers, the tax collectors, the Samaritans, the neurotics and psychotics, those who attempted suicide, the poor people, the beggars, the lepers, those who ridiculed him, those who betrayed him, even his very enemies? Did he shun the politician, the Pharisee, the rich, the educated, the influential? He shunned no one.

Did he accept the man-made walls of separation between men and men? Or did he set up tables of reconciliation instead? Call to mind the Samaritan woman at the well of Sychar, Zacchaeus up in the three, the woman taken in adultery, the Syro-Phoenician woman.

Is the congregation not under commission to be the ambassador of reconciliation? And must not the congregation itself be a reconciled fellowship if it shall be a reconciling fellowship — where the walls of partition have been broken down and where there is neither Jew nor Greek, barbarian nor Scythian, bond nor free, but where we are all one in Christ?

Is it not true that when the congregation exercises its freedom to go out with merely the Gospel, then it will know how to use whatever else it has — money and talent and buildings and power in politics — as "sacraments of its gift of its own life to the world, as tokens of the ministry of Christ"?

These questions are important, because if the congregation is to function as a leaven, it must be brought into the most intimate relationship with the lump in which it is to work.

It was Arthur Altmeyer who pointed out that "There is no such thing as a problem area — we are all problems. The whole community is a problem in a way, and we can't solve it unless we find some way to develop a program of the neighborhood in action. Our problem is to enable the people, both the over-privileged and the underprivileged, to work together and understand one another. We do not have to worry about specific services if we stay with our basic concept of people as people, and neighborhood as neighborhood." How can a congregation be involved in this kind of enterprise unless it is wedded to its community?

What matters most is that one central interpretation of life's demands runs through everything — worship, education, congregational policies, activities. Separately and together they are to proclaim the Gospel. When the liturgy of the church says one thing and the church council says something altogether different, how can the congregation then have a missionary thrust? It is only as the local congregation in its program and structure reflects its faith that the Gospel becomes a reality to others as well as to the members themselves. It can reflect the faith as it incorporates all members with their diverse gifts in the fellowship of those who are fighting the same battles and engaging in the same struggles. Even though each member must face and make his own decisions, he knows that he is undergirded and supported by the body. It is in this sense that every member meets his problems of home, work, and community. Then the congregation becomes a "koinonia," a dynamic community, which in turn suggests congregational solidarity.

"We are changing the world," chant thousands of boys and girls in unison as they parade around Lenin's mausoleum. It is precisely what Christians mean, or should mean, when they gather around the altars of their Lord and say, "We believe in God the Father." We mean, or should mean, "This is God's world, and it is his will to make it a home wherein his sons and daughters can come to the fulfillment of themselves as persons made for communion with him. He wills that we should take the material and let it be moulded and fashioned as the instrument of his purpose. Our lives are pledged that his will may be done on earth as it is in heaven."

Some Affirmations Concerning the Congregation as a Missionary Force

1. I believe that the saving knowledge of God through Jesus Christ is more precious than anything else on earth and that the essential task of the congregation is to keep that knowledge alive and contagious through worship and mission.

2. I believe that the residential congregation is basic, the sine qua non, to the worship, ministry, and mission of the church. This does not disallow, however, the ad hoc congregations, special congregations, temporary congregations, seasonal congregations. Rather, they are complementary to the residential congregation.

3. I believe that the congregation is on mission sent to its community, and that the congregation is the church resident in that community in the measure that it is a community for others, regardless of the cultural, national, racial, or economic changes that take place. The congregation's mission as it confronts its community is nothing less than the salvation of everyone. When that is the congregation's passion, the Holy Spirit breaks through creatively and sustainingly.

4. I believe that creed and the liturgy are merely solemn games unless, on the one hand, they spring spontaneously from a vital communion with God and, on the other hand, draw life-giving substance from the concrete tasks, claims, and interests which are the actual stuff of human activity.

5. I believe that the parish program is, or should be, the connecting link between altar and community, between liturgy and society. To this end the total parish program, together and separately, should proclaim the Gospel. The integrity of the congregation is in serious question if congregational policies, programs, and activities are not consonant with the Gospel proclaimed and the prayers offered in worship. When a congregation becomes concerned with itself and works for itself, it ceases to be God's sign in the community. The persistent and insistent question is, "What do ye more than others?"

6. I believe that every congregation needs a framework of reference in which to see its role — its given mission. Such a framework requires asking questions like these: Is worship central to the life of our congregation? Does the total parish program proclaim the Gospel? Is our congregation the community's most open society? Are we aware of and informed as to the changes and needs and prejudices of our community? Does our congregation provide a forum to discuss community concerns and major political issues? Are customs and practices still in operation that are no longer meaningful? Is our church a place where men find deep friendship, challenging personal responsibility, wholeness of worship, spiritual equipment to face life's tasks and struggles, transcendence of class and race divisions? Are our members in a supporting relationship with one another? Is our congregation in a supporting and strengthening relation with other congregations? Would it make any difference to the community if our congregation went out of existence?

7. I believe that every congregation must take three risks: (a) The risk of exposure — willingness to see itself and be seen as it really is. (b) The risk of failure. Unfortunately, most congregations give up when projects seem to fail, without recognizing that progress is often preceded by failure. The congregation is not called upon to be a winner. It is called upon to be faithful to its given mission. (c) The risk of challenging what it considers to be success. Perhaps it will discover that its vaunted successes are its failures instead.

8. I believe that all the plans and policies of the congregation must be such as to strengthen it for its proper task and to train and equip men for the Christian vocation in their own callings and professions. It is not the duty of the average layman to become a kind of amateur parson. The essential task of the Christian is to serve the cause of Christ in his home and the work by which he earns his living, and thus to redeem into the kingdom of God that given area of the world's life. This is the true work of the church, and the ministry of all believers. What I am here contending for as vital is that the secular tasks of the

world are integral elements in the life of the church, and involved
in the service of its altars. Else holiness is a word with no meaning. The laymen themselves are the material for churchmanship.

9. I believe that every congregation must consider all other
Christian congregations in its community as allies — never as
competitors. This involves an inclusive, not an exclusive, temper,
the tolerance of a truly catholic spirit, not that sectarian com-
placency with which the word "congregation" is too frequently
identified. There can be one justification only for continued
denominational loyalties. It is that the characteristic forms of
experience and interpretation to which, through its historical
legacy, a given denomination bears witness are regarded as gifts
held in trust for the building up of the body of Christ. There
is a wrong and a right approach to this. The right way, as I see
it, is ecumenical — to cherish that which is distinctive in the
tradition which has been bequeathed to us, not with a sectarian
self-sufficiency but as a contribution to the Great Church. To
hug any doctrine to our own bosom as if it were possessively our
own is utterly sectarian. It is completely contrary to our common
confession, "I believe in one, holy, catholic, and apostolic church."

The "church" is people, not buildings. We must restore the
proper balance between the house of God and the people of God.
It should be clear that wherever the people go, there goes the
church. What the congregation does or fails to do depends upon
what is happening in and through her members. The congregation cannot decide whether or not it will affect the life in the
community. It does so by its very existence; by its physical
presence; by its worship, teaching, action; and by the everyday
life of its members. It is the front line, the cutting edge against
the world. If it is to minister, and not be ministered to, it must
take the form of a servant.

The local congregation, whether it be in the heart of the
city, in the suburb, in the crossroad village, is the all-important
all in the total organism of the church, and its worship and
witness of the people are decisive — for or against!

4.

Neglected Frontiers

Lyle E. Schaller **in**

Christian Mission

It is as important for the church to spend as much time and effort in examining neglected frontiers as in seeking out new frontiers. With this thought in mind I have intentionally chosen not to deal with new and exciting ventures in mission but rather with some of the forgotten frontiers which are still beckoning the church for mission.

Evangelism

Perhaps the most neglected purpose of the church is evangelism. This can be seen in many ways and places. Perhaps the clearest is to examine the way churches grow in numbers. Basically churches, like communities, grow in size by two means. First of all, the number of people born into the community usually exceeds the number of deaths. In demographic terms this is referred to as "natural increase." This is the major component in the population growth of America today. It is also the major component in the growth of most of our Protestant denominations. The people born into the Christian families exceed the number of Christians who die each year. Most of our "new members" come from within the family – children of members, spouses of members, and transfers from other churches. In the

Methodist Church, for example, over two-thirds of the 300,000 persons who join a Methodist congregation on profession of faith each year are the children or spouses of members.

The second source of population growth in a community is migration — the number of persons moving in exceeds the number of persons moving out each year. If we apply this frame of reference to the church, we would see two sources of in-migration — transfers from other congregations and persons who join by confirmation and have never before been confirmed members of a Christian church. There are two parallel channels of out-migration — transfers out to other congregations and confirmed members who leave the church for the life of a non-participant. This last group is revealed in our "clearing the rolls" procedures. (Incidentally, it must be recognized that many of those who are dropped from membership for inactivity subsequently do turn up as active members of some other congregation.)

Transfers in and transfers out cancel each other out in our arithmetic, leaving us with new converts from "outside" and those who are dropped from the rolls and go back "outside." The difference between these two totals is the gain — or loss — from "migration." In American Methodism the result is a net loss from migration of approximately 25,000 per year. This total is offset by our growth through natural increase and thus has escaped the attention it deserves. I suspect the same pattern prevails in many other denominations. In effect, our failure in evangelism is partially obscured by our growth through natural increase.

A second aspect of this problem of evangelism can be seen in the large number of our local churches that are not evangelical. They may appear to be faithful to two of the purposes of the church — the corporate worship of God and the purpose of sustaining and upbuilding the faith of the members — but they largely or completely neglect this purpose of outreach. Can a Christian church be a Christian church and not be evangelical?

In a study we are completing in Cleveland the area includes twenty-one mainline Protestant churches. By the most charitable definition I can use, no more than seventeen of these are evangelical congregations. What is the responsibility of the evangelical denomination to which these non-evangelical congregations claim a relationship?

A third dimension of this problem concerns new church development. Is new church development a tool of evangelism? Or is evangelism a tool of new church development? The way many old, established congregations view proposals for the establishment of new congregations I am led to believe that they believe new church development is a program of the enemy and that they see evangelism as a tool of new church development. If they saw new church development as a tool of evangelism, they would exhibit less resistance to proposals for the establishment of new congregations.

Worship

Each passing month finds me more convinced that we are neglecting worship. During the 1958-1964 period, while the population of the United States increased by ten percent, church attendance dropped about ten percent. The new "radical theology" defines Christianity as "an affirmation of the secular world in the style of the man Jesus, and has no relation to traditional church practices such as worship, the sacraments and prayer."[1] Many of us have trouble with this new concept which is gaining acceptance in some circles.

However, let's face it, on a typical Sunday morning well over one-half of the Protestant church *members* in America do not attend any corporate worship service anywhere.

This same neglect of the importance of corporate worship can be seen in the new congregation which builds an eight-room church school as its first unit without providing an adequate physical setting for corporate worship. It can be seen in the practices of many churchmen, both pastors and laymen, who seem to regard worship as an appendage from the past and who place their primary emphasis on social action, Christian education, and counseling.

---

[1]New York Times, October 17, 1965.

On the other hand, I am impressed by the growing interest of a number of people in worship and in liturgy, but I also am depressed by the number of new congregations that appear to give worship a very low place of importance in their planning for building and program.

This may be the most important frontier in our mission today.

Problems of the Clergy

Many observers are concerned about the low enrollment in our seminaries. This, I believe, is merely the headache that suggests a more profound illness.

In a typical year I will visit with perhaps 300 pastors. I am dismayed by the number of unhappy men I encounter — but let me add some of the happiest pastors I meet also appear to be among the most ineffective and some of the unhappiest appear to be among the most effective. My guess is that perhaps one-fourth of the Protestant clergymen I encounter would leave the pastoral ministry if they had an attractive face-saving alternative open to them.

I am struck by the tensions which plague some pastors. Consider the man who serves a church in the inner city and has a sense of mission to the neighborhood, but the non-resident congregation is a "come structure, care structure" group. Or think of the pastor who serves a new suburban mission where the mission board thought they had sent out a new church developer and the people expected they would be sent a shepherd.

I am impressed by the analysis of one minister when he describes the "crisis of unbelief" in the ministry. This appears to be real, to be growing, and to merit attention as a seriously neglected frontier in the total ministry of the church.

Ministry of Reconciliation

Another severely neglected frontier of mission is the ministry of reconciliation. Today, in a society that is sharply compartment-alized on social, economic, racial, political, and cultural lines, there is a need for a ministry of reconciliation. When a delegation of slum dwellers, led by a couple of white clergymen, comes in and deposits a dead rat on the mayor's desk in city hall, the church should be there to help the mayor understand why this has happened, to reduce the degree of misunderstanding, and to turn this event into an opportunity for God's reconciling love to be at work.

There is a need for a reconciling ministry across these compartmental lines — between central city and suburb, between Negro and white, between the rich and the poor, between the haves and the have-nots, between the oppressed and the oppressor — and among neighboring Christian congregations who operate as though each were God's only instrument in that community.

Today the churches appear to be more interested in conflict than in reconciliation.

Church Administration

Perhaps the least important but probably the most neglected frontier in our total mission is church administration. There are too many facets to this issue to even mention them all here, but the list includes the apparent guilt of many denominational executives over not being in the pastoral ministry, the attitude of our churches and churchmen who seem to regard the denominational structures as a necessary evil rather than as a legitimate expression of the church, our failure to provide any effective training or preparation for the men who are called to administrative posts, and the remarkably poor quality of the decision-making process at both congregational and denominational levels. Instead of debating whether we should abolish congregations or do away with denominational structures, I strongly favor improving the quality and performance of these institutional expressions of the church. Let me offer a few varied examples to illustrate this point.

What is the "proper" rate of interest a denomination should charge on a loan to a congregation? Are we really doing anyone a favor by charging a below-market rate of interest?

What is the impact of a denominational subsidy on the giving level of the local church? Does this subsidy usually mean that the level of giving in the local church can — and will — go down by an amount equal to the subsidy?

What is the special calling of the denomination as a part of the institutional expression of the church? Is this different from the special calling of the congregation? Are there non-overlapping areas of concern and competence? Are there some functions which are appropriate for the denomination, but inappropriate for the congregation?

Is it true that the primary reason most of our congregations carry on their work in almost complete isolation from neighboring congregations is sociological and not theological? Does the institutional pressure for a system of vertical relationships in all social structures more than offset the unity which is inherent in allegiance to one Lord and Savior?

What is the authority of the majority in the church? Must the church operate on the basis of consensus rather than majority rule?

Have new tools for decision-making been developed which could be used by the church?

It seems to me that greater attention to some of these old and neglected frontiers will enable us to be more effective as we seek to function on all the frontiers of mission.

II.

The Ministries of the Congregation

5.

The Power

F. Dean Lueking **of**

Preaching

Most of my friends consider the Protestant pulpits to be irrelevant, fearful, and not very scholarly; many in our parish regard the pulpit as harmless and boring.

Woe to me if I do not preach the gospel! (1 Cor. 9:16).

It is well to keep the truth of both statements in mind as we outline some of the key issues on preaching and the mission of the congregation. The first, quoted by Donald MacLeod in a recent article on preaching, can be echoed by each of us. In this age of cluttered communication to the minds of men, it is said that preaching is in trouble. One president of a large Eastern seminary put it bluntly: "Preaching is gone to pot." Ralph Sockman observed in an address last year at Union Seminary that "the warning signals are up that this so-called post-Christian era could become a post-preaching era."

Preaching in an Age of Cluttered Signals

What are the facts and forces behind these statements by men who are well qualified to make them? A realistic look at handicaps facing the ministry of preaching today makes one thing abundantly clear: The pulpit monopoly of audience attention is ended. Today's preacher encounters a rival in every radio and TV station in the land. With unlimited funds at their disposal as well as speakers trained in the arts of persuasion far beyond what a few seminary courses in homiletics can possibly provide for the parish minister, they have effectively dispelled the last remnants of the era of great preachers. Even in the rural American scene the designation of the minister as "parson" is obsolete. He is no longer the "person" of the town, recognized as the best educated and most competent intellectual pioneer. Today's preacher faces in the pew men and women more competent in cultural attainments, and at times even in book theology, than himself. Does this now mean that the preacher can no longer be certain of his vocation as preacher, and that he will do well to turn his energies to institutional or liturgical concerns or to the counseling ministry in which his superior competence can still receive recognition?

The answer to the question is obvious. No, the passing of the era of the pulpit prince in American religious life is not a calamity. We may in fact welcome the new situation in which the preacher cannot so easily regard himself as the darling of an admiring coterie, whose opinion is dutifully sought out on every conceivable subject. The Word of God is not validated by its popular reception in the world. It does not stand or fall according to the statistics of those who assemble to hear it. This must be said in an age which may read all the right analytic books on the irrelevancy of the church in its suburban captive state, and then remain paralyzed with analysis. The probers and diagnosers have something to say and must be heeded, but all the questions about forms and new ministries must lead directly to the purpose of proclamation. "Woe to me if I do not preach the gospel!"

The Word Carries Its Own Authority

For the fact is, God will have his Word proclaimed! He will, now and in every age, sink his Word deep within the hearing of people. Preaching is more than reading the text, though it is certainly tethered to the biblical text! The sermon contemporizes the Gospel, a Gospel which, as merely read Gospel, might have remained safely entombed in the church's historical archives. From a *then,* or "once upon a time," the sermon confronts men with God's *now.* In the sermon Christ himself encounters the hearer, and the "now" in which the preached word sounds forth is the "now" of Judgment Day. To assert this is not in any way to belittle the Scriptures; it is to point to their purpose. The Word of God is not the Word of power and judgment and resurrection God means it to be unless it is preached in fidelity and heard in obedience. When the prophet Nathan, in the familiar Old Testament account, appeared before David and related the story of the poor man's lamb, the discussion to which the story gave rise was certainly not unprofitable, as can be a discussion of a Scripture passage in a Bible class. But Nathan's sermon with its "now" and with its "Thou art the man" came as a thunderclap. Or, to cite a New Testament illustration, when Jesus appeared in the Nazareth synagogue and read the Isaiah prophecy of the coming of good news, we gather from the account that no disturbance was even remotely in sight. It was again the sermon with its "now" thunderclap — "Today this scripture has been fulfilled in your hearing" — which threatened the preacher with martyrdom.

The Preacher: Servant of the Word or Human Whims?

Not every sermon next Sunday, obviously, even if "duly preached," need involve the risk of immediate martyrdom. Yet there is scarcely a pulpit in the land for which Holy Scripture might not furnish a Word of the Lord which, if boldly contemporized, might not bring the hearers into judgment and disturb our ease in Zion. A recent report from a Mississippi minister illustrates the way in which the proclaiming, accosting, demanding, promising word of preaching can be muted and therefore a hindrance to the Word: "Of course I am for brotherhood, but my chief business is to save souls. Now if I preach brotherhood, members will leave and they will be lost. Therefore, in order to save them and keep them saved, I cannot preach brotherhood."

"Members will leave" — that is the testimony of a man's service not to the Word but to the prejudices of those who must hear the Word. Such an illustration lays bare a long-standing ailment that has been nursed along by our pietist tradition. We have neglected the prophets and their courage to address the Word of God to a world where men barter and trade, scheme and connive, threaten and deceive. We have not learned to really know the world in its depth and breadth. Therefore we have trouble reading the signposts of God's work within his world.

The Mission: Penetration of Life as Well as Covering the Earth

The consequences of such things bear directly on preaching and its place in the mission. Because too many of us view the mission geographically rather than sociologically, preaching can shrink down to a harmless veneer rather than flower into a powerful penetration of human lives. If congregations today are seriously threatened by becoming little more than a secularized institution and an inept religious enclave isolated from the social struggles churning about them, it is because the working of the Word of God has been so despised and neglected by pastor and people that the "famine of hearing the words of the Lord" prophesied by Amos (8:11-12) has come to pass. Conversely, here and there throughout the land when the strange story of God's love in Christ for sinners is proclaimed, be it only by fools for Christ's sake, but proclaimed to men where they are in the center of their lives, then God's Word remains in God's keeping. The seed of the kingdom bears fruit. Although the preachers are "like men sentenced to death because we have become a spectacle to the world" (1 Cor. 4:9), they let it be so, knowing that the mission leads men to the kingdom not via triumphal ease but by way of a cross. "The preaching of the church contains, in all humility, our Lord's own activity," Luther said. When the devastating power of that preached Word besieges the favorite illusions and cliches of the hearer, nothing less than an earthquake can be expected.

"Blessed are those who hunger and thirst for righteousness, for they shall be satisfied" (Matt. 5:6). So reads one of the familiar Beatitudes. However, what if there exists no such hunger and thirst in our affluent society, in which "man come of age" accepts the apparent fact that "God is dead"? A hearing of the Gospel may have to await God's breaking the pride of this modern man come of age, God himself preparing a pathway for his Word. The preacher today may have to let that Word, enacted in the events of history and time, perform its work in the lives of his people before his strange message will once more be fully welcomed as good news. Yet, surely there are signs, visible to the eyes of faith, that such a new advent is looming on the horizon.

Mutual Ministry of Pastor and People for the Mission

To be able to read those signs of the Word at work, preacher and people must be in close touch with each other. Each helps the other grasp more firmly the Word that is preached; each can help the other better understand the world for which the witness is meant. In the broad sense of the term, the ministry of the Word is given to the whole congregation. The preacher is, according to Ephesians 4:11-13, one in a group of special helpers sent by God to equip his people – the laity – for ministry in the world. The measure of preaching, therefore, is always the extent to which the ministry is being carried out by the laity between Sundays when they are in the world. This ministry, incidentally, is usually the least known by the preacher himself. To remedy this gap in mutual communication between the pastor and the ministering people, a number of methods are being employed here and there. Some pastors work with sermon talk-back sessions, some with post-service small group discussions, some with weekly sermon text study groups (either elders, officers, members, or any combination of the three). The issuing of parish lectionaries containing sermon texts for all members to have before Sunday as a guide to personal or family worship is another way of strengthening the sense of the whole people of God in any given place participating in the proclamation.

I personally bear witness to the value to myself and those whom I serve to be presently engaged in a systematic effort to visit members at their place of work and inquire with them how their ministry and mission is going. In 100% of the visits so far, it is the first time a pastor has come to them where they spend the majority of their waking hours in order to recognize them as a part of God's mission to his world. The idea that the church is no less the church when outside the sanctuary is theoretically acknowledged by all of us, but little actual time and effort is concentrated on the church on Monday in comparison to the church on Sunday. Here is where we may most appreciate the higher levels of education and competence today's laity possesses in contrast to former generations. The very fact that the layman does read, does reflect, does think, absorb, and understand is a marvelous work of God that must never be resented as a threat. It must be seen as a gift. Like all God's gifts, it can be spoiled and misused by the devil who can create nothing but only twist what we turn over to him. But why cower in the face of that constant temptation? Why not rejoice over the fact that the laity is coming of age in this era when the preacher is no longer the star performer? What counts above all is that the Word of reconciliation is held forth to the world by *all* those commissioned in baptism to be with God in his mission to his world.

The Forms Vary: The Content Is What Counts

I hold no brief for the exclusive priority of the Sunday morning pulpit as the sole and primary avenue of preaching in today's world. I am aware of and call your attention to the work of Horst Symanowski and Eric Mueller-Gangloff of the German Evangelical Academy movement in new forms of proclamation. These men are acutely aware of lonely, depersonalized men and women who may happen to wander into a Sunday morning service and see and hear but never encounter the Word. Symanowski knows from experience that most German working men cannot be dragged screaming into Sunday morning worship. He also knows from experience what happens when a group of workmen, possibly after a midnight shift in the factory, accept the invitation to a face-to-face open discussion that may lead to an opening for the Word to stand in their midst as the demanding, exciting, interesting, and explosive power that it is. When the Word can be heard and obeyed in faith in such a setting, the proclaimer knows it is not a rope of sand that holds the hearers together, but a genuine sharing of the Spirit and mutual watching over each other's souls can take place. Mueller-Gangloff holds that we are at the threshold of a third millennium in the history of the church in which the pulpit sermon is no longer the primary agent of communicating the Gospel. Rather a ministry (and possibly a lay ministry at that) might be emerging in which the servant of the Word is the *Conferencier,* the discussion leader in open dialogue with the hearers. Such a form may be a vanguard sign for the institutional church to heed and follow. The hearer is no longer an isolated member of an audience facing a distant pulpit or an equally isolated and lonely recipient of the bread and wine at a supposedly corporate Lord's Supper. Rather there is a circle of Christian fellowship where each faces the Word with a sense of mutual recognition of the other as a responsible person. The congregation-without-pulpit is still the congregation-gathered-around-the-Word. The pulpit as such is not the issue, nor the sermon as an art form or a formal oration. The preached Word is the issue. What all such new forms of preaching and mission must keep foremost is that the Gospel cannot be arrived at by solitary meditation or by the process of group discussion. At the very most, all that could be arrived at by these means would be the need for such a Gospel. The Gospel is given by the authoritative Word. It is proclaimed. It is a command and an offer. Thus the congregation which gathers about it, whether large or small, whether on Sunday or any other hour of the week, whether in a church building or in a kitchen, is "a congregation of faithful men, in which the pure Word of God is *preached.*" This is the heart of our tradition. This is the best gift we have to bring to the ecumenical church.

So we return to the opening set of statements from MacLeod and Paul. Yes, preaching is a problem in today's world of cluttered signals, but preaching is always problematic. More accurately spoken, it is not preaching that is the problem, it is *my* preaching that is in trouble. The healing of that problem always turns upon the Gospel itself, which is given the church for the sake of the world. We can thank God that we are placed in this very generation. The Word is not one whit diminished for our day. A growing number of laity recognize the ministry for which it empowers them and are asking only to be equipped faithfully and intelligently. The Spirit already has gone ahead of the church into the world to enable the miracle of hearing and heeding to take place. Therefore, our situation is summed up well by Paul: "A wide door for effective work has opened to us, and there are many adversaries" (1 Cor. 16:9).

6.

The Wholeness

Frederic J. Downing **of**

Worship

The church is the people of God who have been called out of the world by God. The church, created and sustained by the Word of God through the activity of the Holy Ghost, the Lord and giver of life, gathers in the form of congregations throughout the world.

The people of the congregation of the church of Jesus Christ are different from other people in the world because of the work they do. To be sure, the people of the church are no different when it comes to jobs and occupations. The difference is due to the fact that every member of God's church is also a priest, a member of a royal priesthood, which offers the sacrifice of prayer, praise, and thanksgiving as it presents itself as a living sacrifice to God. The congregation has a specific relationship to God the Creator, through Jesus Christ. It is from this relationship that a second relationship springs: the relationship with all mankind. As priests we offer to all men the love of God, which alone can restore them, as it has us, to life with God. These two relationships, the vertical and the horizontal, are the inseparable components of worship.

Worship is the purpose of the congregation, for this family of God exists for only one reason, and that is for the glory of God. There is no other reason for becoming a Christian. Joining

69

the church for business or social reasons, or believing that the "family that prays together stays together," is not a proper motive for becoming the church, the people of God. The glory of God is attained only in worship. This is so because worship is the human response to the awesome presence of God. Worship reflects the encounter and confrontation of God and man.

Having defined worship in this manner, we must say at the outset that worship can never be properly contrasted with mission. The reason for this is that both worship and mission are words used to describe the total purpose of God's people, who discover themselves to be involved in God's mission to the world, which God began in Abraham, climaxed in Jesus Christ, and continues presently in the church of Jesus Christ. Christian worship is the celebration of the gracious presence of God with his people, in which the whole person participates in the saving events of Christ and responds to God in union with other members in the Body of Christ. Worship, therefore, is the mission of the church, and our mission as the church is worship.

The Greek word for worship is *leitourgia*, which comes from two other Greek words, *laos* and *ergon*. The meaning of the first of these is people and the meaning of the second is work. Therefore, when this word *leitourgia* becomes a part of the Christian church, *leitourgia* is seen as the work of the people of God. Worship, properly understood, describes the life of the person who comes to faith in Jesus Christ. Whenever we talk of having worship services on Sunday, our usage is improper, for it distorts the real meaning of worship. When worship is not seen as the total life of the new person in Christ, we have much difficulty fitting ourselves into Luther's doctrine of the priesthood of all believers. With worship happening only at appointed times within the church building, we have trouble being priests to one another.

Common usage has distorted the meaning of the word "worship" so that by worship we usually mean a specific rite done at a specific time, usually on Sunday mornings. We have not usually seen worship as our ongoing life in that procession in history which can be identified as the church, the people of

God. So it is that the bricklayer has difficulty in being a Christian, or a priest, or a little Christ as he builds walls during the week. A major problem which continually projects itself into the forefront of Christian life today is this very thing of separating and divorcing our faith from our daily lives. One example would be the actions of some of our congregations which continually preach love, but in fact will not allow certain men to enter their congregations because of the color of their skin.

The Basis for Worship — Baptism

The church, God's family, comes into being because of God's confrontation of man in Jesus Christ. The climax of that confrontation was a death-life experience in which the death of God upon the cross turned out to be victory over the powers and forces of evil. That resurrection victory gives life, or at least the possibility of life, to mankind. All who respond to Jesus Christ as life-giver do so in their own death-life experience, which is the basic dynamic of baptism. It is in baptism that the old part of us is put to death by God, and he brings forth new men, who from this moment on live a life described as worship. Baptism becomes more than being adopted into the family of God, and it becomes more than a citizenship in God's kingdom. Baptism becomes the formula of this new life identified as worship. Just as our Lord's dying and living are basic to the faith, so our daily living and dying experiences are the basic pattern of God working in us. For instance, we allow Christ to put to death certain sinful and weak parts of us when we make use of the confessional. This death experience is then followed by the resurrection experience of Holy Absolution. This death-life pattern is the pattern of the new life called worship, and it is the pattern for the mission of each congregation.

God's Church Gathered for Service

The church is the corporate fellowship of believers bound together by a common calling, a common life, and a common destiny in Christ. It is for this reason that a Christian cannot live in isolation from other members of the Body of Christ. The corporate gathering of God's people is a most important thing. It is like a family reunion, and the spirit should be the same. The early Christians never asked the question whether they should or should not go to church, for they realized that without this most necessary service from God to them, they could not survive.

No one can be helped unless he admits the need for help. For instance, a man with a broken arm will never go to a doctor until he decides he needs his arm repaired. So it is with the congregation. Unless we state our need for God, we will not be looking for him to come into our lives, nor will we be ready for him to come. This is the genius of the general confession done by the gathered family. We are not only admitting the mistakes and sins of the past week, but we are also admitting who we are; namely, very weak persons who find it impossible to keep God's Word by our own power. In the general confession we are like the sick man, admitting our sickness and asking the divine Physician for health.

The gathered people of God also hear the Word of God in the form of lessons and sermon. The Word of God is always a two-edged sword, convicting us of our shortcomings and forgiving us for our shortcomings. God both tells us how weak we are and gives us instruction as his very own children.

From hearing the Word of God, which is designed to disturb the comfortable and comfort the disturbed, we go to the second high point of the liturgy, the Lord's Supper. This sacred meal has always been viewed in Lutheran circles as a special sign and assurance of forgiveness. However, we must not lose sight of the other purposes of this most sacred meal. We must regain, somehow, the truth which tells us that this is the only food which can empower us to keep God's Word. This is done, of course, by reconnecting us to our only power, Jesus Christ.

Having looked briefly at some of the dynamics of the liturgy done by the gathered church, or congregation, let us turn to the necessity and beauty and wisdom of the Lutheran liturgy. From time to time we hear cries about the antiquated nature of our liturgy. Oftentimes the reasons for such a demand come from pastors who feel they are dealing with people whose backgrounds are such that the people will not like what the Lutheran Church has to offer. To allay such fears, permit me to draw from personal experience. The parish which I now serve is predominately Negro, and the parishioners, for the most part, were not familiar with the Lutheran liturgy or any liturgical tradition before coming to Holy Family Church. However, they have developed a love for the liturgy to the degree that when we attempted recently to use some of the best Negro music as a setting for this liturgy, the resulting responses from parishioners ranged from disgust to horror. Let us beware lest we discard the genius of the Lutheran liturgy for the sake of popularity.

What are some of these points of genius preserved by the Lutheran liturgy? There is, first of all, the genius of preserving the healthy tension between the prophetic and the priestly. We know from the reading of the Old Testament that the roles of prophet and priest were always in tension as balancing factors in God's Old Testament church. In present-day American Lutheranism, which has been greatly influenced by American Protestantism, the Sacrament is omitted, except on Communion Sundays, and the sermon is preached every Sunday. The result of such radical surgery on the Lutheran liturgy results in a faith which is heavy on knowing the right answers. Our danger, then, is that we develop a religion of brain, and our faith may be dangerously close to being only intellectual. On the other hand, if we, like the Roman Church in past years, removed the sermon in favor of the sacrament each Mass, the service would take on a magical flavor, and we would begin to get the idea that the service is a place to come to get our tanks filled with "grace," a sort of magical, protective stuff. In reality the service has never been a time of filling tanks but a time of complete overhaul. What we are saying is that the prophetic office of the Word and the priestly office of the Sacrament are of such a nature that they must be held in tension.

One of the advantages of our Lutheran liturgy is that it is a demonstration of the coming of Jesus Christ to man. Everytime it is celebrated in its entirety the service tells the Christmas story again. It is for this reason the preacher may feel secure. Each one of us who has ever stepped into a pulpit, or who ever will, will some time or another be guilty of heresy. This is bound to be because we are human. The genius of the liturgy is that even though on a given Sunday we preach false doctrine the people are guarded against it by the liturgy itself which clearly proclaims the central message of the Gospel.

Still another genius of the Lutheran liturgy is its demonstration of the oneness of Christ's Body, the church. What a tremendous display of oneness we have in the reception of the blood of Christ from the chalice in a day when those outside of the church are having difficulty living next to one another. What a tremendous display of oneness the church makes when manager and laborer, Negro and white, teacher and student, kneel to become one in Christ.

Our traditional liturgy encloses the basic requirements of worship given by our Lord himself, namely the preaching of the Word and the eating of the Lord's Supper. And the liturgy does this in a tried and tested structure, which has been put together by many of the saints.

God's Church as It Returns in Family Units to Homes

There are other instances at which the family of God gathers for corporate life. However, these are of such nature that they cannot be identified as events attended by all at the same time. Yet, on the other hand, they are attended by more than one of the families of the parish. I am now speaking of such things as the study of God's Word, during which time the mutual conversation allows for the grace of God to come in a very real way to all who participate. Martin Luther pointed out that this mutual conversation of believers is especially effective in the flow of grace to God's people.

Having stated that the church is by nature a corporate body of believers who share a common life and destiny, we must now make some provision for the individual family units of this corporate body as each unit returns to its individual home. Any family or personal devotions must grow out of the corporate life of the church. In one parish the pastor carefully selects Scripture readings for each day of the week, which will prepare the individual family unit for the coming Sunday and its theme of worship. These readings are included in the Sunday bulletins, as is a common prayer theme for the week, which each individual family member will be praying daily. An integral part of worship is family worship, which is not divorced from the worship of the corporate body of Christ.

God's Church Dispersed into the World

It is impossible to disconnect this aspect of worship from that of either the gathered family of God, as a congregation, or from that of individual families and their worship.

We have referred to the basic pattern of Christian life as the death-life experience, first encountered in the entrance rite of baptism. Now we shall see how this works by viewing the family gathered about God's altar, and then watching this same group disperse into the world for continual worship.

The very coming of a child of God before the altar of God should in itself become a life experience. It is such a life experience in our community, for the majority of our people come out of the bare concrete block walled rooms of high rise apartment living. Such mass produced, low cost, high rise buildings can lead to a real death experience of seeing oneself as just another of some 18,000 people living in the same, identical apartments, or of discovering that you are known to the office only as a number. It is the death experience of the de-humanizing tendency which such living produces. Others in the parish come out of homes infested with roaches, and in some cases rats. Oftentimes the linoleum is 10 layers thick, paint on the walls is pealing, roofs leak, and plumbing fixtures do not work.

Our church building is simple and small, but our people thank God for its beauty. Just being able to say this is my church can be a valid life experience for many. Let us make no apologies for the beauty of our church buildings, but let us, as did ancient Israel, use nothing but the best in the construction of our houses of worship. This in itself can become a meaningful part of a person's life of worship. Church buildings are missions. Buildings and missions have become integral parts of worship and cannot be placed before us as if the modern Christian must make some either-or selection between the two.

This life experience of entering the church building continues as the other members of God's holy family gather about us. It is life to know that we are surrounded by people, who are sinners to be sure, but who know it, admit it, and strive with the help of God to change, to love, and to care. How different this is from the deluge of people we usually encounter in the rat race of the business world or the fraternity rush. It is at this point we suggest the best in Christian architecture, an architecture which says something about who we are as the church by the fact that such architecture is there as a necessary aid in our life of worship. One example is the use of the free-standing altar, which not only allows the celebrant to face the people during the celebration of Holy Communion, but which also allows the people of God to receive their family meal while completely surrounding the table of God. We have no need to fear beauty in our worship, for it says much to those who see the ugliness of life all around them.

Another much neglected but very healthful aspect of our worship should be mentioned. This is the very Lutheran practice of private confession, which Dr. Luther valued and recommended so highly as a necessity in the life of every believer. It is in the very dynamic of this sacrifice-sacrament that the death-life experience is relived. That sinful weakness which tears at our very existence as children of God is placed out in the open by confession where this sinful part of me can be put to death. Once this confession has been made, once this sacrifice of self has been accomplished, life can again be experienced in the sacramental action of holy Absolution.

The life having been received through absolution, we turn

to another life-death experience, the hearing of God's Word, whether it be in the reading of the lessons or in the sermon, which is God's Word applied to the modern situation. We discover that according to God's Word we are dead, for we become identified as Pharisees and outcasts. The feeling which results is inadequacy, which is a real death. But as we listen further we hear we have life because of God's action toward us in Jesus Christ.

This brings us to another death experience, the offertory. The offertory seems to be the most neglected part of our liturgy in the Lutheran Church, which is understandable when we think of Luther's heavy emphasis upon *sola gratia.* So let us take a very careful look at this action of the liturgy, in which we, for the first time in the service, give ourselves in response to God. The money which we place on the altar and the bread and wine which we place there are symbols of the work we have done with God's good creation. In other words, these are symbols of our very lives. The complete action of the offertory, however, is threefold. Not only do we place money, bread, and wine upon God's altar for God's use, but also we lay there the needs of all sorts and conditions of people in the world. In these three actions we ask God to accept what we offer as something useful to him in the building up of his church and the increasing of the kingdom of God. However, we are really doing something much more basic, for we are in these actions offering ourselves as living sacrifices to God. We are saying, "Here I am, God, willing to be used by you in your mission." The offertory is the death of each one of us individually. We lie sacrificed upon God's altar, an offering which God may use as he sees fit.

This complete sacrifice of death experience is then followed immediately by the life experience of the Eucharist. Having stated our willingness to be used, God now comes to us and places in each individual the very body and blood of Jesus Christ. This meal is essential for us to be able to do the work of God's people, or to say it another way, to continue our liturgy. It is in this most holy of moments, during the reception of Jesus Christ, that Christmas is celebrated all over again, for God, who once became man in the person of Jesus, now places himself very really in us, even though we are unworthy.

It is precisely at this moment we so often think of worship as ceasing, for in just a few minutes after the reception of the body and blood of Jesus we sing a recessional hymn and walk out of the church building. If it is true that worship ceases upon our exit through the doors of the church building, then we are to be pitied, for we have missed the entire message of the Christian faith, which insists that a godly life necessarily follows the reception of Christ. Is this not what James is saying to us when he states, "Faith too, unless it has works, is dead in itself. For just as the body without the spirit is dead, so also faith without works is dead"? If worship is not our entire life in Christ, whether in the church building or in the supermarket, then we are in effect saying that our faith has no bearing on what we do from day to day in life.

When the Christian walks out the doors following the service he is a new man — forgiven and empowered by God's service to him in Jesus Christ to serve God and his fellow man. Is it not the very reliving of this saving event, or to say it another way, the very reconnecting of the person to the saving event of Christ, which solely empowers him to worship and therefore to carry on the mission of the church? There seems to me to be no more real way of being thus connected than by having the body and blood of Christ placed within my body.

Let us pause to see what we become because of the action of God upon us as we are gathered for his service. We become the extension of God's incarnation, the church, the Body of Christ, or as Martin Luther puts it, little Christs to the world. Wherever we are, then, our worship continues and identifies us as members of a congregation doing the work of the church of Jesus Christ. This means the Christian butcher worships as he cuts meat, and the Christian worships as he demonstrates against the injustices of our land by marching in civil rights protest marches. We worship when we cast our votes for presidents and governors, as well as in the politics and campaigns which come before elections. We worship while transacting business and we worship while crouching in the crude foxholes of Viet Nam. We never cease to be what we are, namely people seeking to bring the love of God to bear upon a wounded mankind. Our life becomes a process of watching for opportunities which can be used to bring men back to the love of God.

Worship is the mission of the congregation, for it is the word which describes the life of a person who dares let Jesus Christ call him out of the world into a group of people who are bound together to extend the purpose of God. Without gathering regularly about God's altar to hear what God would say to us, or to receive the food which alone empowers us to worship, without these necessary actions, we cannot be the church. Only when God places his Christ within us will we care about worship at home, or will we care about carrying Christ into every decision of our lives. Only with Christ living in us as Savior and Lord will we care about our fellowmen and whether or not they know God. Without worship we have no mission, and we could not be the church of Jesus Christ.

7.

The Encounter

Melford S. Knutson

of

Education

The congregation has sought to prepare her members for mission by a system of Christian education that has been limited to Sunday school and confirmation instruction. Many congregations have taken quite seriously Proverbs 22:6, "Train up a child in the way he should go, and when he is old he will not depart from it," failing to realize that these words were spoken at a time when the education of children was the chief responsibility of the father. Many congregations, too, have built their structure on the premise that if they get the children they will eventually get their parents. They have failed to realize that Isaiah 11:6, "a little child shall lead them," is a prophecy regarding the child Jesus. As a result our young people leave the church by the thousands after confirmation, and when they become parents they use the church for giving their children Sunday school and confirmation instruction, who in their turn follow the same pattern.

It is strange that we could fall into this kind of rut, because we do make the parents solely responsible for the child's Christian nurture at Baptism: "I charge you that you diligently teach him the Ten Commandments, the Creed, and the Lord's Prayer, that as he grows in years, you place in his hands the Holy Scriptures, bring him to the services of God's house, and provide for his instruction in the Christian faith."

Even in our instruction of children we make a great deal of Exodus 20:4-6. "You shall not make yourself a graven image, or any likeness of anything that is in heaven above, or that is in the earth beneath, or that is in the water under the earth; you shall not bow down to them or serve them; for I the Lord your God am a jealous God, visiting the *iniquity of the fathers* upon the children unto the third and fourth generation of those who hate me, *but showing steadfast love* to thousands of those who love me and keep my commandments." We have memorized these verses ourselves, and we have insisted that every boy and girl in the confirmation classes know them from memory.

After we have given the charge to a father at the baptism of his child, and after we have warned every pupil of the judgment that comes upon negligent fathers and the blessing that follows to loving, obedient fathers, we leave it there and go on with our own academic system as though he did not exist. It is as if we are saying, "If we can get these children away from their parents, and fill them full of our teachings, we will train a better generation of parents." But this has never happened.

Lord of Love

Too often the church has assumed the responsibility for the religious education of children and has disregarded the commands that God has given to a child's father. When God made man he called him "Baal," that is, "Lord." He was created to be lord over his wife, his children, his cattle, his property, and his household. When he misused his privilege and became a slave driver, he was called "Adhon," which means "tyrant." "Baal" is used in the same sense that Paul uses it in Ephesians when he refers to Christ as Lord of the church. He is a Lord of love. Christ loved the church so much that he gave his life for the church. Paul admonished men "to love their wives as Christ loved the church." He is the strong one, and his wife is often referred to as being weaker. He is the head of the family because everything has to have a head. He is the breadwinner, the protector, the aggressor in making the right physical, intellectual, and spiritual adjustment between him and his wife. He is the private tutor of his children, the one through whom the love of God desires to flow into his children. Who could possibly be more concerned about a child than the parents of that child? Of course, the child's mother is important, but definite commands and responsibilities have been given to the father, and we must not allow anything to detract from them. The church's chief responsibility is to help the father to be the kind of "lord of love" over his family that God intends he shall be.

When God wanted creation to continue he made man his partner. He created him "just a little lower than the angels" and made him the pro-creator. Man plants the seed for the birth of every human being, without which there is no human birth. The importance and responsibility of this are emphasized in the birth of Jesus. God did not want man to cooperate in the birth of the God-man. He was to be the "only begotten" Son. The Holy Spirit planted the seed in Mary, and Jesus the Savior was born to save all people from their sins. But in the birth of all other human beings man plants the seed. He is a partner with God in creation. This places a high and holy responsibility on man, and the church must help him to learn to know who he is. We have done well in helping man to realize his responsibility for providing food, clothing, and shelter for his family, but beyond that we have done very little for this key person in God's kingdom.

Communicator of the Covenant

God gave the covenant to Abraham, the father of Israel, as we have it recorded in Genesis 12. He said it had to be kept alive by repeating it verbally as well as all the other great acts of God through his people. The Ten Commandments were given to Moses as recorded in Exodus 20. Instructions regarding marriage were given and are recorded in Deuteronomy 7. Certain feast days were set up to commemorate God's acts and promises, and the fathers were given a command to teach these important, personal matters to their children. All elementary education, and especially that pertaining to the personal concerns of religion and sex, was the responsibility of the father. There was no school in existence in Israel until after the exile, and then the synagogue school was only an aid to the father. The Jews have been more faithful to this command than any of the Christian denominations. Their divorce rate and sex delinquency rate are the lowest. Perhaps our high rate of divorces and the entire sex revolution have been caused by our failure as a church to help the father to carry out his responsibility to his children in these personal areas where he is the personal one in their lives.

Religion Is Also Caught

William Barclay, in his book *Train Up a Child,* says there are sixteen passages in the New Testament that are related to teaching a child "reverence," "respect," a sense of "awesomeness," and "holiness," and every one of them places a great responsibility on the father. We complain a good deal today that children have no respect for God or man, and we criticize the church and the school for failing to train them in this area. Harold Taylor in an article, "What the Family Isn't Teaching" in the *Saturday Review,* May 18, 1963, says, "The direction of learning is from emotion to thought to expression in words, symbols, or symbolic action of some kind — not the reverse, as most educators think. . . . If we begin by assuming what educates deeply is the immediate experience of a child within each situation in which he is placed, then the family is what educates the most and the soonest, since the child is born into it. The personal relations within the family begin working as educational instruments as soon as the child is born. Here are contained values of all kinds — political, moral, social, aesthetic, spiritual that suffuse his life." The old cliché "religion is caught as well as taught" must not be lost. If a child sits next to his father, "the strong one" in his life, the "head" of his family, he catches something that will never depart. The hour of worship is the only hour in their lives when a deep sense of reverence and respect can be communicated. The father should be encouraged to take his child to worship at the very earliest age.

Martin Cohen wrote an article, "A Man Is Daddy" for *Redbook*, June, 1965, in which he offers evidence from extremely well balanced sources that the American father is the greatest man in the life of every child. In one church a study was made that showed that where the father worshiped with his child, eighty-five per cent remained faithful to the church and where the children participated in Sunday school and confirmation without any interest shown on the part of parents only fifteen per cent remained faithful to the church.

On Being a Father

One more biblical concept which we have overlooked and which we must revive is the name "father." Through repentance and forgiveness God becomes our loving Father who watches over us, cares for us, and is always concerned about us, and we are caught up in the "fatherhood of God." Paul says in Ephesians 3:14, "For this reason I bow my knees before the Father, from whom every family in heaven and on earth is named." The name father is given to man after God. He is to be the little father of the earth. When a person is asked by a child to tell whom God is like, the answer should be "like my father." The church's responsibility is to help him to be the real priest in his household that God wants him to be.

The basic and fundamental principle for the educational program of the congregation in preparing her members for their ministry in the world is to make sure that the schedule for worship gives the image that the involvement of the father is imperative. He should be told by the church that his presence with his child in worship is the very least that can be expected of him. The normal pattern for every child is that his father is indispensable for his physical welfare, and the church must help him to realize that he is indispensable as far as his child's spiritual and intellectual development is concerned.

The church school classes for children and adults should

always follow worship as a natural order. Classes for adults should be Christ-centered and relevant to the family, the vocation, the community, and the world. Helps and suggestions should be given constantly to parents to make them aware of countless agencies in the community that can teach them to bathe a baby, plant a lawn, or understand a teenager.

The church must also provide materials for a father that can acquaint him with his task and responsibility and give him helps for carrying out his role. The wide variety of occupations and professions occupied by fathers makes it necessary to produce helps for a father so he can carry out his role that is lived in the most unusual circumstances of life. Devotional materials written for the father as the priest to use for his family, and simple teaching materials for table talks that have a man's flavor are needed.

If the church can help a man to be a man in his own kingdom, his sense of mission will break through in every area of his life. In one large congregation that pioneered in this experiment, where church attendance and Sunday school attendance were way above average, the worship attendance increased by seventeen per cent and the Sunday school attendance by five per cent. More than that, the men of that congregation are alive, alert, responsible, and sensitive to mission in the community and to the needs of the world.

8.

Benjamin A. Gjenvick

The Selflessness of Social Ministry

Without more than acknowledging the continuing discussions of the nature of the church which have accompanied her history in this world, it is not inaccurate to suggest that throughout this history an enduring characteristic of the church has been the localized grouping of people for worship, edification, fellowship, and service — the congregation. The current discussions on the congregation, examining anew its essential definition, appear to be raising at least four basic categories of questions: purpose, structure, task, and method.

In these terms we should consider whether the defined mission of the congregation should in fact include diakonia, social ministry, as a basic purpose. At the theoretical level this question may have been fully settled for all of us. The day-to-day practice of the typical Lutheran congregation suggests far less certainty.

Preaching, teaching, and the administration of the sacraments occupy secure positions in the definition and practice of a Christian congregation. Diakonia (service) appears to enjoy no such certain position. Generally, training, organization, and direction comparable to that for parish education, for example, simply do not exist for social ministry.

Before we draw unwarranted conclusions from this situation,

however, it is essential to examine the nature of social ministry in the contemporary congregation and its surrounding society. To do so, I first return to the question of purpose.

Essential Ministry

The biblical witness, theological reflection, and substantial historical and contemporary congregational experience all affirm that diakonia, service, or social ministry is an essential component of the congregation's Christian ministry. Worship, including preaching and administration of the sacraments, teaching, and fellowship become self-centered and self-serving exercises, unless they issue in Christ-like concern for fellow men and concrete helpfulness which expresses that concern. The essential Christian purpose of the congregation must, therefore, include in its definition service — social ministry.

Christian social ministry is rooted in the realities of human need and in the God-given imperative to acknowledge and serve need. As over against non-Christian religions and philosophies and sub-Christian understanding, the biblical witness is clear: God is responsible for and involved in the totality of material and non-material creation. People who acknowledge and worship such a God share his concern with the whole of life. Non-material religion, devoted only to saving men's souls, is sub-Christian. Congregational practice, faithful to Christian truth, recognizes and serves the totality of life in all its relationships. All the needs of men are the proper subjects of Christian activity.

There are various ways of identifying and classifying human need. At bedrock, needs appear to reduce to two large categories: one — food, shelter, clothing, and such modern extensions of these as medical care and transportation; and, two — relationships, including family, friendship, neighborhood, community, national, and international relationships.

The congregation which is obedient to Christian truth must acknowledge that none of these needs in all its intricate extensions lies beyond the range of Christian concern. Further, that obedience to Christian imperatives requires an address to these needs, not only in word but in deed. Social ministry is Christian concern properly addressed to human need through Christian service and social action. The purpose and mission of the congregation require social ministry for their fulfillment.

Basic Tasks

From the above it follows that Christian social ministry requires two elements held together continuously and simultaneously: one — Christian faith, including love and obedience; and two — knowledge, understanding, and skill. Without the first element social ministry is somehow less than a true Christian expression and lacks the character which derives from repentance and forgiveness — redemption from egocentricity. Without the second element social ministry becomes sentimentality, blundering, even hurtful, unrealistic, and irrelevant to the hard, complex, trying nature of actual human need.

Social ministry which includes both these elements faces specific tasks. The first task is to seek to know, to uncover the essential features or norms of a God-pleasing society. If this appears as an impossible assignment, the preparation of a utopian design, a more limited objective requires at least an effort to achieve ever clearer understandings of Christian norms and values. While we may not in humility and with due respect for our own human uncertainty find it proper or desirable to address the world with our suggestions for rearrangement of the social household, our own efforts ought to be informed by our contemplation of what a God-pleasing society might be like, granted the present and developing stages of technology, and we should disseminate and demonstrate the Christian values we discern.

A second task that must continuously accompany the first is that of learning about and understanding the social arrangements for meeting human needs, bodily and relational. This task calls for discovering how individuals and society function, change, and are influenced and moved.

Social ministry in the congregation's life includes service and social action. In light of what has been said above and the discussion which follows, service and social action are two inter-related functions which are results of Christian concern.

Social ministry as service means efforts initiated or carried out by the congregation to supply the bodily or relationship needs of people. Social ministry as social action means efforts directed to encouraging or changing the ways in which society meets or fails to meet these needs.

Structures for Service

It is instructive to see first the structural means through which service and social action can find expression. The first structure, if we may use that term with certain liberty, is the Christian individual. I am endlessly impressed by what the solitary, informed, committed, courageous, and dedicated Christian person can accomplish. The various spheres in which his life moves — neighborhood groups, political party, profession with its complex of groups, service clubs, informal social groups, etc., provide channels for service and social action. They offer milieus in which Christian values and purposes may be given lively expression.

Within the congregation, existing men's, women's, youth, and special purpose groups, such as those organized for parish education as well as the regulatory groups — deacons and church councils — provide structures for service and social action. Increasingly congregations may decide to organize social ministry groups. When this is done, care must be taken to assure that the congregation does not assume that in the activities of this group all of the social ministry responsibilities of the congregation have been discharged. Such groups should be seen as the focus of effort to mobilize the entire congregation (or as many of its members as possible) and all of its structures in service and social action.

Perhaps an illustration may be useful to give this idea concrete reality. A social ministry committee might catalog the human resources in a congregation that could be applied to encourage and assist workers caught in an industry's move from

town. Or a committee, becoming aware of many community
teenagers excluding themselves from the church youth group,
might encourage that group to examine its attitudes and program.
To this examination it might suggest that the group apply specialized social group work and psychiatric knowledge available in
the community.

Thus the social ministry committee becomes a sensitizing
group: it takes human needs in the congregation and community
as its special subject and seeks to relate the whole resources of
the congregation to these needs.

The congregation-as-a-whole offers the next available structure. Browne Barr in his Lyman Beecher lectures, *Parish Back
Talk*, recounts a congregation's address to the problem of open
occupancy. Both closed-to-the-press and public discussion of this
issue resulted in deepened understanding of the Christian message and the specific problem, and their interrelationship. The
results of this encounter, though not spectacular, included a large
newspaper advertisement written and inserted by a doctor-lawyer
in the congregation supporting the ordinance.

It is commonplace for whole congregations to support church
social service agencies with interest, prayer, and financial gifts.
In their most adequate forms these agencies employ highly qualified professional staffs, who apply sophisticated knowledge and
technique in response to complex human needs and problems.
Too often, however, these agencies work in isolation from the
congregations which create and sustain them. Wherever this
happens, the agency clients, the congregations, and the agency
staff — all are poorer.

There is not the time to discuss the significance of the church
social agency, but one observation is useful to this discussion.
The church agency's basic distinction is its relationship to the
church. Increasingly, this relationship must freight a heavier load.
The significant knowledge, understanding, and skill in helping,
acquired in intensive daily effort devoted to troubled people,
must be made to flow into the congregation for use by pastors
and laity. The congregation, in turn, must develop fellowship
among its members which communicates the realities of accep-

tance and love that have their origins in the experience of God's forgiveness. Thereby troubled people can find not only the therapy offered through a specialized agency, but also the sustaining strength of Christian fellowship.

The congregation's relationship to government and private social agencies requires considered attention. The vast growth of government social welfare activity means that many needs, once served by families, the church, or voluntary groups, if at all, now receive government intervention and service. Furthermore, government is turning to the church and other private groups to conduct services, using tax funds, notably in the so-called poverty program.

The ethical and professional standards under which government and private agencies function require informed scrutinizing by the church. Whenever a congregation accepts government funds for a special service, it must assure itself that it is capable of fulfilling its obligations, and that its own purposes are not compromised.

Continuing the examination of Christian structures for service and social action, we move beyond the individual congregation. Here we find ourselves on even less familiar ground. It appears to me that Lutheran congregations are generally oriented to their own life and activities and to those of the church bodies to which they belong. Not too often does an individual congregation join with other congregations in a community or area to deal with a need requiring service or social action. Similarly, synod or district service and social action efforts have yet to develop broad and deep-running congregational participation.

The mission of the congregation, expressed through social ministry, promises significant fulfillment as congregations discover each other and their common communities. Ecumenical relationships become a practical necessity when human needs become a burning reality to Christian consciences. The necessity of developing practical service and social action activity in response to need can redeem such relationships from endless discussion. That the integrity of confessional position need not be lost in such common efforts is amply illustrated by the Greater

Milwaukee Conference on Religion and Race. The religious forces of the community have found it possible, without compromise, to testify to a common concern for human rights.

Church bodies and church councils can contribute notably to the clarification of theology, human needs, social structures, and their functioning. Congregations and their sub-groups, with study and experimentation, can develop practical applications of these resources to actual human needs.

The sheer glory of social ministry in the witness mission of the church is wonderfully portrayed in the following project. A layman, an architect, in whose life there throbs the presence of Jesus Christ himself, with his wife and his Sunday school class started a coffee house. Located in the basement of their inner core church, this coffee house has attracted 200 teenagers. Many of them are rejects of the schools and of community social agencies. The large response has provoked a crisis because the facilities can comfortably accommodate only sixty. In an effort to deal with this shortage of space, he sought the gang leaders in their homes and neighborhoods. A white, suburban, professional man seeking delinquent gang leaders provoked a startling response. "Who are you, a detective? What's Joe done now? What trouble is he in?" Then, another boy among the gathering throng said, "Naw, he ain't a detective. He's the man from the coffee house!" In this trust, in the identification of a friend, you can hear the echo of voices from an age ago. They talked about a man whose origin and identity were uncertain, too. Some called him "the carpenter's son from Galilee."

9.

The Fullness

Arthur R. Simon   **of**

Fellowship

Christian fellowship and the mission of the congregation belong together. The single point I want to make is that koinonia cannot be detached from the mission of the congregation, although in fact this is so widely attempted that it has become the accepted pattern of congregational life. People who have no intention or understanding of being in mission cannot be in fellowship either.

The mission of the church is to the world. The church in mission describes the servant-church, giving its life ceaselessly and compassionately for the world. If a congregation ceases to engage in mission and instead becomes a self-promoting, self-serving organization, then no matter what sort of theology or piety decorates that congregation — and it may be very orthodox theology and very respectable piety — koinonia has been replaced by a cheap imitation.

Exhibit A: A congregation in the city is frightened and baffled by a changing neighborhood. It seems quite natural to most of its members to build a new church in more pleasant surroundings away from the dirt and noise and strangeness of neighbors they never got to know. Changing club facilities seems to them not only justified, but a responsible step forward, completely compatible with their understanding of the church. They are doing it, as they say, so their fellowship will grow. Others in the congregation, determined to stick it out with dear old St. Jonah's, begin welcoming neighborhood people to be part of "their" church. Bit by bit the Sunday school is integrated and at last even the church council. Then comes that great and awful day when prominent members of St. Jonah's realize it is no longer "their" church, and so they too abandon it, along with the godless city, to the newcomers.

Exhibit B: A church is more crowded than usual because it's communion Sunday again. People go to the altar to break bread and drink the cup together — or more accurately, to receive individually stamped wafers and separate glasses together. But the "together" doesn't mean much, because people are lined up shoulder to shoulder as folks who don't know each other and don't care about each other—or if they do, they do so often for reasons that are not related to the meaning of this sacrament. Still they call it communion.

Exhibit C: A lady dressed in $80 worth of clothes, leaves her attractive suburban home, steps into a late-model car and drives across town past three other churches to attend a meeting of the Women's Missionary Circle. There she sips tea with her friends, hears the pastor speak to the group about mission work in Japan, and assembles $1.59 worth of things she has brought along for a world relief kit.

In the situations I have described—the fleeing congregation, the people attending communion, the lady at her church club — I have said nothing critical about anyone's theology or personal morality, as those are usually understood. But where is koinonia? Fellowship has gotten to mean what happens when like-minded people get together to participate for a while in that sphere of life called religion and demonstrate their loyalty to the religious enterprise. If there is any conscious connection between this and the mission of the church, it is usually made in terms of expanding the religious enterprise so that *more* like-minded people can get together and participate in that sphere of life called religion.

Real Church Work

We churchmen have fostered this situation in a host of ways. Let me isolate one particular way. We have given laymen the impression that their ministry is to the institution. We have told them that full-time Christian service means being a professional church worker. Church work is what you do at church or for a church committee. Laymen are summoned to be "kingdom builders" — perhaps by being asked to pledge hundreds for a new education wing, and nothing for civil rights; or by being asked to attend a church supper, but never asked to attend a union meeting; or by serving on a stewardship committee where men, unchallenged, remark to one another that the poverty problem would be solved if we didn't make it so easy to live off welfare. We may call that kind of participation "fellowship," but the whole context is one that bends the Christian in on himself, so that fellowship becomes a kind of self-indulgence rather than a resource for serving in the world.

Perhaps it is good to remember that one of Luther's favorite targets was ecclesiastically concocted good works that had nothing to do with the neighbor or human need. He maintained that service to God was always service to the neighbor. Have we not in our day revived the heretical practice of urging not human need but the churchly enterprise to be the occasion for Christian service? And are we not then twisting the meaning of mission which permits koinonia to become a reality?

Authentic Koinonia

If there is to be koinonia, a real sharing in the body of Christ, then there must be a constant rhythm, like the beating of a heart, of the gathered people and the people dispersed in the world to serve. In his book *The Congregation in Mission,* George Webber shows how the East Harlem Protestant Parish tries to live by this rhythm. He says that the people of God should gather for word and sacrament, for worship and study and let death be spelled for most organizations within the congregation.

We suggest that the present predicament of the church demands that most of these groups be given up for the sake of mission. If the justification for the organization is fellowship, then God may grant that a far deeper understanding of fellowship will be discovered in the Bible study group.*

The fellowship of special interest groups tends to be something less than koinonia, Webber suggests. "A missionary congregation does not need a women's missionary society, but women engaged in mission."*

All this might suggest that if the lady who drove past three churches to the Women's Missionary Circle had instead been working with neighbors for integrated schools, or for open housing, or in some other way had been involved in discerning human need and responding to it, then she might have found a different reason for gathering and a different set of circumstances prevailing. A group of Christian women similarly engaged and feeling the need for mutual support and prayer might ask one another questions like, "How did your ministry go this week?" or, "How do you understand this particular problem?" or, "How can I celebrate the presence of Christ with respect to this situation?"

Crossing Boundaries

It is the nature of the church to be crossing boundaries, as the Book of Acts reminds us. That book also reminds us how difficult it is and how much the Holy Spirit has to prod us. Nevertheless, the church in mission is the church crossing boundaries. It is likewise the nature of koinonia that it reflects the crossing of boundaries. Therefore we need to ask ourselves what the implications are of planting most of our new congregations in places where people are carefully separated from those who are not racially, economically, and culturally similar. To what extent *can* koinonia reflect boundary-crossing under such circumstances? And is it not imperative that the church, for the sake of mission and for the sake of koinonia, begin a massive crash pro-

---

*George Webber, *Congregation in Mission*. Abingdon Press, 1964.

gram to tear down the terrible walls of residential isolation that have made our nation sick? The church is uniquely equipped by its theology, its geography, its numbers, and its resources to do this job rapidly and effectively. The real question is, does the church *want* to be in mission and let a more genuine koinonia flourish?

If we are to take the New Testament seriously, then we cannot understand koinonia apart from the Lord's Supper. "The bread which we break, is it not a participation (koinonia) in the body of Christ?" We call this sacrament "communion," but rarely does one refer to it as "fellowship," perhaps for reasons that are obvious. The New Testament practice suggests that we need to let the Lord's Supper resume a central place in our common life, and that it be renewed as a real celebration, a joyous family feast. What we need is a kind of transubstantiation — that is to say, if people find themselves together in this sacrament for reasons that are accidental rather than substantial, let the substance of their drawing together be transformed. That transformation cannot take place unless people relate the celebration of this sacrament to their mission of compassion in the world. But within the sacrament are riches of matter and actions and words to do just that.

We have often used this logic: If we can get people to experience koinonia, then they will get on with their mission. But the pattern and direction of our congregational life have introverted our sense of mission and prevented fellowship from emerging in the only context which the New Testament knows for it. Now it is clear we must engage in mission so that the gathered life of Christians can be a genuine fellowship in the body of Christ.

10.

The Enthusiasm

Erling H. Wold **for**

Evangelism

If there is anything that hangs heavy over a parish pastor's head, it is the seething restlessness of people in this age of discontent. Everything is coming loose that can. Our personal tensions mount because of our fears over our society. The church no longer deeply affects the lives of Americans. Dr. Will Herberg of Duke University says, "Christianity amounts to little more than a big spirit of friendliness and a willingness to support churches, providing these churches demand no real sacrifices and preach no exacting doctrine."

Second, we are plagued by the deeply disturbing fact that we are not reaching the world outside with the Gospel. Our primary results seem to come from the already conditioned and the concerned, those who already want to come.

If George Sweazey is right in saying, "Evangelism is every possible way of reaching outside of present church membership to bring people to faith in Christ and membership in His church," we are not doing well at all. We begin to feel an intense longing for some kind of spiritual revolution. The very needs about us demand it. Even in the university area, Harpers Magazine last February said that the muffled snarl that comes from our colleges and university campuses is the sound of unhappy college students enrolled in courses with a swelling suspicion that they're

98

being gypped. They're not getting good teaching, and their discontent is due largely to this. And so an editor said students are in revolt again. Well, our world is like this toward the church, too. Our Samarias and uttermost parts must include the disinterested, the disenchanted, the disturbed, the forgotten. We ought in a series of discussions like these become our own severest critics, stinging ourselves into vital action.

Our Savior said, "You shall be my witnesses." Fulfilling this is the core imperative of the church. Everything in a sense begins here. This is our operative framework. Here we discover the greatest secret of all: that God can use me. But my whole person must be wrapped up in it. He wants me totally involved. For to be a witness, an apologetic, a credential for Christ means that my whole set of values takes its heartbeat from this reality. Graham's newest book is called *The World Aflame*. This demands a church aflame. It means you fighting to be his man; reincarnating what he said: "I have come to send fire on the earth, and I burn with passion till it be ignited."

This is the type of witness that is implemented in evangelism. *Evangelism* is how you become his witness. This is your program, your procedure, your profession. It's only a part of your witness, but it's vitally significant. Sweazey says it's the church's biggest task. Your witness is all that you do. As Kaj Munk said, "It's how you treat your neighbor." But your evangelism is how you lead another to Jesus Christ and help tie him to the body of Christ. Therefore, evangelism is *how to;* that's what the church is for. We can no longer live in the twilight zone that Einstein mentions, that we have a world of perfect means and confused goals. We are the worshipping body of Christ, committed to show forth the praises of him who called us out of darkness into his wonderful light.

How can we accomplish this? The finest summary that I know comes from a friend, Dr. Louis Evans Jr. from LaJolla, California. He was called a year or more ago to serve an older church that now has three distinct types of members. Its young people, its scientific community centered in the University of California in that area, and its senior citizens. Dr. Evans says succinctly that he has three basic assignments. One, calling men to Christ; two, helping those called to develop and mature; three, asking them to go out to become the healing, cleansing persons of Christ, setting captives free. In short, you can say, Come, Get ready, Go!

Come

Everyone needs a central identification. Each one must be led to say, "I belong. I belong to Jesus Christ." To say this as deeply and profoundly as little Miss Marie. I love that little story that came from Bishop Berggrav. Marie was taught for confirmation in a home in the hills of Norway where she could not make it to the regular confirmation classes. Her mother, therefore, taught her at home, but she came for her catechization to the church, on the day of confirmation. She and the rest of the students were lined up, one per pew end in the cathedral, and the bishop came to ask each one a searching question. When he came to Marie, for some unknown reason, he said to her, "Marie, Jesus doesn't love you." He said the entire congregation was electrified as if they were in the presence of eternity. But this shy little mountain girl looked down for a moment at the floor, and looked him flush in the eye and said, "Oh, but I believe it anyway." It is this fantastic conviction that knows it's loved that must permeate everyone that's called to belong to Jesus Christ.

And this, without question, begins with the professional clergy. The ministry is unquestionably the key. Dwight L. Moody said that if you want a conflagration in the congregation you must have a fire in the pulpit. So often I sense that our sophistication, our seeking for intellectual niceties, our lack of power keep us from any longer stirring anybody with any kind of inner fire. We become happy with the status quo. How different Christ! I often think of that passage in the New Testament which says, "Jesus cried out in the temple." He was aflame with it. There is no soul pure that isn't passionate. The congregation stirs restlessly if it isn't called to a new faith and a new fervor. Sweazey said, "No church ever slides into evangelism; it's always slipping away from it." Everything in human nature is trying to tear you and your church from the practice of evangelism. Unless you have something that is going to take it and thrust it into the center of your consciousness, you are inevitably going to let it go. So I ask myself, as you ask yourself, "Is my devotional life alive? Am I a formalist? Has my love grown cold?"

So we need a new flaming commitment, a raw, bruising connection with the living Christ. A man said through many years across many luncheon tables, "I've asked the best established Christians I've met this simple question, 'Is Christ real to you?' I hope God will forgive me for the embarrassment, the confusion, and the stuttering I've engendered." The way to God always begins with heart-deep repentance. Our commitment to him must be so deep we're willing to pay the sacrificial price, we're willing to relate to individuals no matter what their color might be. We've got to reach to become what he is — for God. Come! That's the first call of God.

Get Ready

There's no question about the necessity of preparation for the laity. Dr. Frederick Ohlert says that 95 percent of the members of the church have never won anyone to Christ. We have an unhappy conviction that this is true, and this must be caught first as it's taught. Dr. John Mackay once said, "Nazism had fire; communism has fire; the church needs to catch fire." We've got to encourage one another to really live by faith, to expect a living response. I was vice chairman of the Graham Crusade in our city two years ago. One thing I learned effectively from this vast effort. The people who came largely expected something to happen. They came praying, expecting people to get converted, expecting people to come, expecting that this whole vast enterprise that cost about $1,000,000 would be financed, expecting that cell groups would be formed and prayer groups would be a part of the entire effort. This expectancy paid off. God still honors faith. I heard three Sepulveda psychiatrists in our town say they can tell when they accost a patient in his room whether he will be healed or not. They said, "We sense a circle of defeat or a circle of faith. Some just have it."

Therefore we must help our people catch the inspiration of the involvement. They must be brought to say, "I am a member of the body of Christ." Members must know what it is. There is an interesting Syrian woman who comes to our church. She has a tremendous fearlessness when it comes to witnessing. She moves into Veterans' Hospitals, talks to people across counters, and even stops to talk to people in cars parked by the curb. She had an accident not long ago when her husband ran into a large piece of concrete on a major highway. The car was upended, and they were barely able to crawl out of the broken doors. Thirty-five people came hurrying up to see if they could help. Indomitable Mary reached into the broken wreckage and took tracts out and began to pass them to the folks who had come, and said, "Jesus Christ saved me from death." But though she has come to worship with us for two years, she hasn't brought a soul into the fellowship. She never attached anybody to the body. It's the church, the gang that Christ left to finish his job, that must have the priority.

Then the congregation must reexamine itself. I was interested in the statement by Woodrow Geier, editor of *Trustee*. He participated in a student recognition service, where young people did the unexpected. These young people wanted to find first-hand convictions, become aflame with those things that are real. Instead of saying nice, harmless things, they told the congregation why many students leave the church today. The church's moralism and teaching, its banality in worship, its hesitancy and compromising on social issues, its lack of theological sophistication, its preoccupation with statistics and machinery, its inability to identify with needy people — these came in for criticism. When the service was over, there were gasps and sputters. Wasn't it shocking that the pastor allowed his pulpit to be used for chastisement of the church? But one layman said afterwards, "Ours is a free pulpit. These students showed more sense and spunk in a few minutes than the laity has shown around here the last fifteen years." Dr. Geier said the layman didn't defend all that the students said, but he had caught the note of anxiety, hope, idealism, and responsibility burning inside their hearts. They really wanted to know. Shall we find an organization, a structure, for a congregation? It seems to me this is imperative. It's one of the many means. Witness is a lifetime relationship, but evangelism means techniques of reaching the unreached for Christ. The techniques must be purged perpetually but still used. In the seven giant megalopolises that are going to be formed in America in the future, and in all the rest of our larger cities, 90 percent of the people won't come on their own. People must be trained to reach them face to face, person to person. Everything else is a conditioning technique. Christians must penetrate a community. They must get into homes, offices, make contacts where people actually live. We are called to reach people.

George Sweazey says, "The things that have marked the great turning points in my life usually happen in groups. It's true about my own family," he said, "and in some of the sessions we had in the dormitories when I was in college and some of the student conferences. It wasn't the fellow who came and asked, 'Young man, what are you doing with Jesus Christ?' It was rather in some fellowship where something warm and Christlike began to glow from heart to heart and the glow that began to kindle me. As far as my own autobiography is concerned, those have been the great moments in my life, and I think perhaps in our church life we haven't made enough of that."*

Go

Years ago when I was at a student conference a brilliant speaker wrote in a book that he autographed for me, "Christianity is a life to be lived, not discussed!" It's the doing of it that matters. Doctrine isn't much good unless it's put to use. Proclamation? Sure, that's seed-sowing. We follow the patience of the Savior who perpetually kept tossing seed. We don't stop preaching nor witnessing by word of mouth.

---

*George Sweazey, *Effective Evangelism*. Harper and Row, 1953.

Demonstration: that's seed-cultivating. That's Paul mending his tents, analyzing the passerby. That's Chaplain Boyd saying, "You'd better take evangelism seriously." Why not discuss with the unchurched in situations where the Bible is studied in relationship to the daily newspaper or the current magazines? This means looking for a point of contact in terms of another person's experience, concern, and interest. This means being a Christian at home, and being a convicted, convincing Christian in the life I live. It's having a passion for people like Jim. He's struggling to make a mark in the movie industry. I spoke at a Christian fellowship where he came and sat on the floor. He talked to me briefly after the service. He came to see me again some weeks later in my office. He told an interesting tale. His life was filled with uncleanness. One afternoon shortly after he'd heard the Gospel he was driving down LaCienega at Third. Suddenly his heart began to constrict, a voice inside him began to scream, "You're gonna die, you're gonna die. You're gonna die in your sin." He left his female companion in the car at the curb and began to run helter-skelter down the street. And the voice kept plaguing him. He didn't die that day, but a few nights later at 3:00 in the morning he was suddenly awakened by the same terrifying experience. It was then that he began to pray. In that awesome hour Christ became his Savior. He sat in front of me in my office, face just aglow. He had only one passion, to be a servant for the Christ who had redeemed him. "What can I do, Pastor?" he asked. "What can I do?" I said, "Two blocks down there is a bachelor about your age. His past is filthy, too. He's full of fears. He's inhibited. He can't sleep nights. But he's afraid of God. Your voice can likely penetrate him. Why don't you go find him?" Without a moment's hesitation, off Jim went. The next afternoon I was at a busy intersection. There was Duane in his car turning the opposite way. He's the one I sent Jim to see. Duane smiled broadly and screamed across the traffic, "That man you sent, he came! He waited for me till 3:00 in the morning!" He came — that's evangelism. That's the mission of the church. God's man, going.

11.

Robert J. Marshall

The Co-Partnership with the Church Body

Some developments in the church presage a diminution in the role of the parish and a more prominent place for the territorial church (*Landeskirche* in Germany) or church body. The trend is most evident in Western Europe, where attendance at worship in the parish church has dropped to a frightening low point. In this situation the territorial church discovered that it could approach structures in society more effectively than the local parish and that it was also able to set up structures in which it could reach persons who had ceased to attend the parish church. In America the church body has also experienced an expansion of its functions. Though the parish structure has not been threatened to the extent noted in Europe, many ask whether the time will not come when a parallel situation will develop. This question provides the proper setting for any discussion of church body and congregation.

Mission Through the Church Body

Recently so much attention has been given to the mission of the congregation that we might easily lose sight of the mission of the church body. Yet the church body and its work developed

105

as a result of the impulse to mission. To use terminology which is much in vogue today, we may say the church body developed from the impulses to be a servant church and to be identified with life in the world. The organization of the church always develops partly under the impact of the *social structures* of the world. When these structures are too large or too distant for the congregation to reach, a larger church body is needed.

This phenomenon can be seen in the relationship with *government*. In the First World War, the need for military chaplains gave rise to an inter-Lutheran agency which could more adequately represent the church to the government than could separate church bodies, let alone separate congregations. Similar offices have served for institutional chaplains at both national and state levels. Campus ministry provides another example. Social action beyond local efforts also requires jurisdictional units of the church to match those of the state. In all of these instances the church body or related agencies can serve as the best channel for the mission of the church.

A second structure of the world important to the organization of the church is *marketing areas*. Economic patterns determine population movements. When freedom of movement extends over a whole nation, the church body should be nationwide in scope to allow proper planning and church development. To minister to its own people or to all people, the church needs to be able to draw upon resources wherever they exist and to deploy them for American missions wherever the need is.

Certain current *sociological factors* work to the advantage of the church body and to the detriment of congregational strength. Though most church members still yield their first and greatest loyalty to their congregation, they are wooed away by what could be purely secular forces, which must be dealt with by supra-congregational power.

To begin with the most obvious, we may speak of the *mobility* of the population. How many persons belong to the same congregation for a whole lifetime? Patterns of identification are broken by attendance at college, enlistment in the armed forces, failure to return home after these dislocations, response to opportunities and attractions in various parts of the country or the world, business transfers or dislocations from company mergers, industrial transition — but the problem is evident enough without expanding the evidence. A congregation ministers to a parade.

Obviously a congregation might rely on being the "friendly church" though such a characteristic, be it actuality or only publicity, holds less attraction for the younger generation than it does for my own. Or it might rely on the need for pastoral services, though this can become fairly superficial with regard to funerals, weddings, and even baptisms and confirmations. Counseling needs are prevalent and less superficial, but in this day of burgeoning science, the physicians and psychologists attract most of the business. The congregation can still rely on a native religiosity among American people. Some will emphasize it most for their children and chiefly desire a good church school, but considerable numbers accept Sunday worship patterns. Yet here we must recognize an identification with something more than an individual congregation. The person conforms to a national pattern, a habit of behavior, and a point of view developed by the whole church. This is my point: the local congregation is dependent upon a milieu which it cannot create or maintain by itself.

Not even a church body can dominate the scene in pluralistic America. Current ecumenical developments are far too slow for many, many people; and many, many more have long ago unconsciously adopted a common-denominator religion. Nevertheless, denominational organization continues to serve a useful purpose, and the church body accomplishes some of the ends demanded by a mobile population. To mention a system for transferring membership is to consider one of the less significant factors. Of greater importance, the church body provides direction for worship and parish education. Sufficient uniformity results to help a wandering church member feel at home in a new congregation. A church member has been known to choose a congregation for the musical setting it followed in the service. Other ways in which the church body serves the Christian life and the congregation can best be considered under other factors that are still related to mobility.

Mass communication, together with technology and industrialization, has produced the mass society. The result can be seen in the strong tendencies toward conformity and fadism. The desire for standardization appears in the church even among people who often resist it. When a congregation gets into trouble, it will often express the wish that the church body would have a rule to solve the problem. Under such pressure, as a matter of fact, a considerable body of legislation has grown up. I am continually surprised how readily people will accept rules, often more readily than they will accept reasoning on a debatable point.

Though we may lament the "nation of sheep," and hopefully we will work to transform the sheep, the church would fall short of its commission from the Good Shepherd if it did not engage in the use of mass media. Only the church body has the resources and the influence to break into national networks and press syndicates. In large metropolitan areas, a single congregation seldom makes its presence and work well enough known to compare with the impact of the church in small towns. Cooperation between congregations is required to attain adequate attention for the church. Television stations require Protestant denominations to work through councils of churches for a degree of fair distribution of time and space. In addition to the church body's production of programs and publicity, its encouragement is often needed before a congregation will use communications opportunities.

Modern man's desire for anonymity opposes congregational fellowship. When this fact was developed at an evangelism conference, one evangelism chairman came forward after the discussion and reported that he could not see what was wrong with anonymity; he enjoyed it. So do most city dwellers, to some degree. People who move into the city either experience a great loneliness or a new freedom. The latter usually takes over as people realize they will not be subjected to small-town gossip. As long as they conform enough not to make themselves conspicuous, they will be required to accept a very minimum of responsibility. Why identify closely with a group of people which would perpetuate the old burdensome patterns?

Once enmeshed in urban living, the mechanized regularity of life, together with the superficial encounter with vast numbers of people, creates a need for privacy. Urban man seeks release from pressure by withdrawal, or by indulgence in activities which break conformity barriers. For many urbanites, the motivation becomes very weak for increasing primary relationships by active participation in the life of a congregation. To the degree that they feel the attraction of religion, they prefer to practice it as a private cult. They are happy to slip in and out of a worship service without being noticed. If they can avoid responsible involvement and still retain a sense of identification with their traditional denomination, they are satisfied.

Anonymity is served by *fragmentation*. A person can remain anonymous because he associates with people in several isolated groups and so avoids intimate acquaintance with anyone.

Society is divided into many smaller societies. The most obvious practices of segregation are also the oldest. Criminals have been ostracized from primitive times. In antiquity some forms of illness also called for separation from normal associations, but the modern hospital collects vast numbers into a world of its own. Higher education segregates persons for a number of years of their lives. Other education or work or recreation develops unstable communities for portions of each week or each day.

The church has responded with an increasing number of chaplains. Specialization in modern society has led to specialization in the church. Chaplains in the military establishment, in prisons, hospitals, schools, and an increasing variety of institutions, have become forerunners to industrial missions, night ministries, the Christian "presence" in high rise apartments and office buildings. No one sees the end of the demands upon church bodies to assume responsibilities shirked or delegated by congregations. When a new situation arises, the cry sounds forth, "There ought to be a man (a specialist) to take care of it."

To a great extent individual initiative is being replaced by *organizational management*. No longer does the inventor work in the isolation of his shop. Instead, laboratories house teams of research specialists. Though personal qualities equip a man for leadership, the executive exercises little individual decision. He weighs the reports of task forces, and consults with department heads. The decision-making process involves a complicated web of authority and communication. When a mistake is made, it becomes difficult to place the blame because it resides in no one person. Causation depends upon a host of relationships.

The church is sufficiently incarnate to share the organizational structure of its world. The Albert Schweitzers are few in any age, and a sufficient multiplication of them would have produced greater chaos in world missions than existed. Today the demands of governments in underdeveloped nations require working through organizational channels. Need for adequate training further advances the importance of the church body, or some other body. World missions is but one example of the forces at work upon the church.

Mission in the Congregation

With so many forces disrupting congregational life, can it survive? Are there reasons for maintaining the parish structure? Can the congregation be strengthened to fulfill the mission of the church?

From a broad perspective, the parish deserves recognition as a *convenient administrative unit*.

A person does not need to be an administrator of a church body to appreciate the organizational utility of the parish. To establish some semblance of parish boundaries is essential to good relations between neighboring congregations. I say "some semblance," because boundaries ought not harden into barriers. Church members who move out of a parish can benefit from retaining membership in it, if they remain active in its functions. This way they will be able to sustain one well-established group relationship instead of losing it. On the other hand, when a man loosens old ties anyway, when participation in the old parish life weakens, a person should identify with the new parish. He benefits if a congregation near his new home recognizes responsibility for its neighborhood. The congregation can accept parish boundaries to define its area of primary responsibility. Within this area it can work intensively with an effectiveness that would be dissipated by a wider diffusion of energy.

In America, where the church must support itself, the parish has had an advantage it did not possess in Europe. The congregation has been a self-supporting unit. Though it may have become an expression of self-interest and self-serving, the congregation has had few competitors for its ability to raise funds to maintain itself. Motivation lies close at hand. The contributor receives pastoral services, a building for his use and a program which he can help to design, and possibly appreciation and recognition for his gift. Consequently, the American congregation has forces working for its preservation that were not so available to the European state churches which relied upon taxation.

Yet an increasing proportion of parishes are not self-supporting, even in America. The factors mentioned earlier create conditions which a congregation cannot master. Congregations in the inner city, congregations in the depopulated countryside, congregations a-borning in new residential areas, congregations overwhelmed by new growth in universities, industrial complexes, and recreation areas, all these look to the church body for aid. In spite of mushrooming administration in the church body, however, the parish remains a convenient administrative unit.

Aid to support congregational life is not misplaced because it can serve as a *nursery for primary group relationships*. At this point I must admit I may be resorting to dogma. My thought is influenced by the church's long entrenched dependence upon parish structure, but even more by personal dependence upon primary group relationship. Admittedly, in an age when secondary acquaintances dominate an individual's experience, the church cannot ignore them. This is one reason for the recent emphasis upon relating faith to public life. To limit concern to private affairs means restriction to an ever smaller segment of human life. Even a family tends to lose its primary relationships as the members are separated a great deal of time. Possibly, the future will eliminate primary groups. Maybe God intends to develop personality types yet unknown. Then a dogmatic encouragement of primary groups would prove futile and the congregation could not be defended.

Within the limited vision allowed by experience, however, I wish to champion the congregation as a nursery of primary relationships. Members should have the opportunity to become well acquainted and to share confidences. For this reason, they should not be forced to break ties with a congregation when they move out of its parish boundaries, unless they cannot maintain close relationship with it. Congregational life should include a great variety of activities to bring members together in a wide gamut of experiences. The congregation may again become the center of life, if it serves as the one institution dedicated to nurturing primary relationships.

The congregation offers, further, an opportunity to create *a diverse community*. While in the past the congregation tended to embody a homogeneous group, with a separate church for each nationality, some parishes developed a pride in the number of different nationalities which were included, and more recently, others have dedicatedly pursued racial integration. For some people, the church offers the only experience with integration. They have moved to the suburbs as Negroes arrived in the old neighborhood, but by continuing their membership in the parish, they worship, study, and work with the newcomers. In this way the church incorporates residential diversity.

With less accomplishment, the church has begun to seek a second type of diversity. We may call it functional diversity, for the church wants to serve people not only in family and neighborhood functions, but in work, education, politics, and recreation. In this effort, the church may strike a sandbar, which will require throwing the congregation overboard. Maybe the church needs worker priests, industrial missions, park and resort chaplains, night ministers and campus pastors who are not attached to congregations. Maybe life will become so fragmented, the congregation in America will suffer as badly as in Europe. As the work week grows shorter, people will be away from their residences for longer and longer week ends. Travel, moving, and multiple residencies already weaken the residential parish. Possibly, however, congregations will assume new roles. They may accept responsibility for all who enter the parish for any purpose — work, education, or recreation, as well as residence. Then the congregation would attain a functional diversity.

If the congregation is to work in new functions, it will need encouragement and sometimes subsidy from the church body. Indeed, some have already benefitted from such help. With residential diversity, the church body helped by policy statements, study conferences for leaders, guidance from boards and departments of the church, and financial grants. The same is underway for functional diversity. The congregation may yet prove the church's best instrument for mission by becoming a diverse community.

In its diversity, a congregation may find a distinctive role as *a study center.* Kirchentag and Evangelical academy can more readily gather persons of the same occupation; but the congregation can unite its variety of people to penetrate common ethical and theological problems. The residential parish provides a natural locus for attention to family, neighborhood, school, local government, human relations, personal attitudes and beliefs. An increasing number of congregations are rising to new opportunities for small group study, cell groups, week day schools, forums, and retreats. Since study makes possible an involvement in depth, it is an important aid to primary group relationships. In a day which fosters depersonalization, conscious efforts at understanding are needed.

Rapid change calls for education to aid adjustment in new situations. The point is demonstrated by the tremendous amounts spent by industry for training and retraining. In meeting the need in the church, congregations have received new curriculum materials and organizational guides from the church body. Fortunately, the proper boards and departments have promoted the best techniques as well as up-to-date lessons; they have served as a clearing house for gathering new ideas, encouraging experiments, and disseminating information; and they have engaged in continuing research to keep abreast of changing needs. Through the church body congregations inform each other of their experience and strengthen their educational function in the mission of the church.

If unaccompanied by service, study can lead to undue introspective analysis and negativistic criticism. The congregation may serve as *an activation center*. Especially if the congregation develops primary relationships, it may help solve the problems of motivation experienced by large segments of the population. Such motivation can transcend the manipulative techniques prevalent in commercial and political promotion.

Congregational activities may include time-honored functions for socializing, ministry to the sick and needy, and efforts at evangelism and stewardship. Today social action will also have a place. Congregations will need to decide when they should participate in public affairs directly and when they should instead be satisfied to stimulate individual members. In our pluralistic society, the church does not need to perform all functions. Neither do church members need to be related to just two agencies — church and state. Intermediate associations serve a valid function. Without them, the church would become far more institutionalized than it is. Whether the activity takes place within the structure of the church or outside of it, the inspiration can come from Christian faith, nourished and instructed within the congregation. The program will often benefit from guidance and encouragement by the church body.

As a convenient administrative unit, as a nursery for primary group relationships, as a diverse community, a study center, and an activation center, the congregation is worth fighting for. In every function, the congregation receives support and help from the church body. To fulfill its mission, the church needs the national and international comprehensiveness of the church body, with the attendant accumulations of influence and resources. It also needs congregations, with their local concentrations of personal involvement.

12.

The Capacity

Hoover Grimsby **for**

Cooperation

"To live is to change." This statement by William Gladstone is as relevant today as the day it was first spoken. The recurring theme which is found in practically every daily newspaper, weekly magazine, and new book on religion is that of change. We are indeed living in a time of tremendous change. It is not the fact of change but the pace of change that frightens us. The causes are multiple and complex. Urbanization, population explosion, affluence, automation, cybernation, space shots, and mass communication have all had their individual and combined effect upon us. We are still reeling under the impact and there is no prospect of anything but greater change in our future.

It is crucial, therefore, that we ask ourselves the question, "In this world of change, has the local congregation changed, especially in its relationships with other congregations?" Change for the sake of change would be disastrous, but change for the sake of renewal can be of tremendous significance. The image which the local congregation presents to the community reveals much with regard to its own nature.

Congregations in Isolation

The first image which the local congregation has given to the community as a whole is that it stands in practical isolation from any other congregation. If rugged individualism is a virtue,

115

our local congregations have excelled to the point of perfection. Consciously or unconsciously, each congregation has had a tendency to become over the years a denominational, cultural, nationalistic island.

This was brought severely to my attention several years ago when, in considering a call to the great city of Chicago, I visited the other Protestant churches in the neighborhood, asking the staff personnel what they knew about this particular Lutheran congregation, which was their geographical neighbor. The reply which they gave was rather startling, "Oh, that church never has anything to do with us. All we know is that they are a group of Norwegians that love to come together, worship, drink coffee, and go home and have nothing to do with anyone else." This candid description was not only humbling, it was humiliating. It unfortunately was the unvarnished truth. It was a congregation in isolation. Too many of our local congregations have become cozy cubby-holes of the complacent converted and have had little or nothing to do with others; yes, even of the same breed and brand.

At a meeting of some national church executives it was discovered that the most consistent bedrock they encountered as they mined the field of genuine change was that of the autonomous power of the local congregation. In a world which has become so interrelated with change, the individual congregation can ill afford the luxury of isolation. The church in Chicago, Milwaukee, or in any city in the whole wide world can no longer isolate itself. The local congregation has to overcome the temptation of separating itself from the other congregations in the community and of going its own way, which may look successful for a moment, but can only end in frustration, loneliness, decay, and physical death. Congregationalism in the sense of each one going it alone is a suicidal path.

Congregations in Competition

In a sense, every congregation is in business — the King's business. Because there are varying synods and denominations represented by other local congregations in the area, there will always be competition for the loyalties of the same people. To a minimal degree, the presence of other congregations can serve the purpose of wholesome competitive concern. When, however, this concern reaches the point of denominational or synodical rivalry, then certainly the kingdom of God as a whole loses. Examples of this competitive rivalry are too numerous and heinous to even repeat. We can only repent and confess that we have sinned against each other as local congregations of the same or varying Lutheran tradition.

Congregations in Mission

Living and working in a world which has "come of age," the church at the level of the local congregation must also come of age. It can ill afford to be seen by the pagan world as an adolescent, and at times an infant, playing its games of isolation and competition. The world will grow weary with such antics and discard the church as being irrelevant.

If the local congregation is to fulfill its destiny as a local segment of the Body of Christ, it must indeed clarify its vision concerning itself and others and renew its sense of mission. The church is God's servant. It is the Body of Christ in which he continues to be present. It is Christ's agent with a mission to perform at his command and by the power of his Spirit. The church as a local congregation exists, therefore, for one purpose: namely, to fulfill its mission, its calling under God. The church as a local congregation cannot dare to lose sight of the truth about its existence: namely, that it has been gathered and is being sent by its Lord. As a Chosen People, the members of the local congregation are nothing apart from the One who chooses them. The church's mission is God's mission. His love and righteousness are not only the central message of the church, but its motivating power and ultimate goal and existence. It is by God's love that the church ministers, and it is for the establishment of God's righteous kingdom on earth as it is in heaven that it spends itself. As Paul states in his Letter to the Ephesians, "We have been destined and appointed to live for the praise of his glory."

The local congregation cannot reduce itself to purely an external organization where responsibility is easily depersonalized and avoided. It must become the Body of Christ with each member a living part and the total body with all of its members working in harmony with the whole.

Congregations in Cooperative Service

As a local congregation renews, reviews, and relives this concept of mission, it can no longer afford to live in isolation and competition, but it must for reasons of its own spiritual and physical health relate itself to other congregations which are fellow-members of Christ's Body in the community. The message of the church is the Good News that "by One Spirit we were baptized into one body and we who are many are one body, for we are partakers of the same loaf."

Now, then, can we stand before the world and say we love God but we do not love our own brothers? Immediately we will be confronted with the charge, "You call yourself the communion of saints, but where is your holiness?" If there is any place where we ought to reaffirm this oneness, it is by good works of cooperation, it should be at the level of congregation with congregation. Not only on the level of synod and denomination, but on the level of the Body of Christ, which includes all who call him Lord and Savior. Let us examine a few areas of cooperative mission where a congregation can work with other congregations, synodically, denominationally, and interdenominationally, all to the glory of God and to the extension of his kingdom.

Congregations in Relation to Other Congregations
at the Synodical Level

Milwaukee, Wisconsin

The Southern Wisconsin District of the Lutheran Church—Missouri Synod has established a planning council for the inner-city of Milwaukee to achieve a new measure of cooperation between inner-city congregations and the district.

While the planning council will recognize the basic scriptural principle of the independence of the congregation and its final right to take unilateral action, the council will not only serve in an advisory capacity, but in the interests of good stewardship, will promote multi-lateral planning and action, always seeking mutual understanding of the problems involved and the voluntary consent of all parties to the actions agreed to. The council will attempt to utilize in the inner-city ministry whatever old forms of church work may be found practical, and exploring new forms for their feasibility and value.

This inner-city planning council is a practical follow-up to the results obtained from the Milwaukee planning study.

Washington, D. C.

The Maryland Synod of the Lutheran Church in America has approved a project whereby eight Washington churches will work together forming the Cooperative Lutheran Parish of Washington.

The Rev. Daniel L. Pierotti has been called to serve these eight LCA congregations in their relation to the community. His concern will be the restructuring of church programs to make them relevant to present-day needs, including the possibility of direct social and political action. He will be responsible to a board made up of two laymen and a pastor from each of the cooperating churches.

One measure of the new warmth that marks the Washington district is the number of pastors who turn out for each other's special congregational events. The dedication of a new church or parish building, the installation of a pastor, or the recognition of a major anniversary brings fellow-pastors to share the occasion and extend fraternal greetings.

Intersynodical Relationships

Baltimore, Maryland

The most pretentious and far-reaching project in inter-Lutheran circles relating congregations together is the Baltimore

Lutheran Urban Church Planning under the direction of the Rev. Thomas J. Weber. This project represents a five-year program which has reached its halfway point. All of the 119 Lutheran congregations (ALC, LCA, and LC-MS) of the Baltimore metropolitan region are organized through representation into 13 neighborhood strategy committees. Emphasis is placed on the fact that the Baltimore Lutheran Urban Church Planning is process-centered rather than project-centered in its basic orientation.

It is the process whereby the facts, factors, forces, and future of society are assessed in light of the mission and purpose of the church with the view of accomplishing that mission most effectively and faithfully. The neighborhood strategy committees form the context in which the planning process operates, and this neighborhood process is coordinated with the efforts and concerns of the committee on Baltimore Lutheran Urban Church Planning, which is composed of national, regional, and local representatives from the major Lutheran bodies.

"To be sure," Pastor Weber states, "specific projects developed as a result of this process orientation, not because they were conceived, initiated, and energized solely by an individual expert in urban church mission, but rather because of an aroused, enlightened, and interwoven concern on the part of the church itself to overcome the complexities of urban mission." Each neighborhood strategy committee is composed of the clergy and two lay representatives from each Lutheran congregation of the neighborhood area. One neighborhood strategy committee proposed a cooperative social ministry program which was adopted by the congregations and in turn called a social group worker to assist the congregations in developing their ministry to the diverse racial, cultural, and economic groups of the churches. Another has opened a community concern center which operates with a volunteer staff. Other neighborhood strategy committees have discussed fair housing and conducted a common campaign for the good neighbor pledge. Others are delineating primary areas of mission responsibility.

Joint councilmen's dinner meetings have been sponsored by

most of the neighborhood committees. Other projects which have been developed are a "huddle-house" evangelism program, a cooperative summer evening teen school, and a cooperative summer school day-camp program for inner-city children. Pastor Weber concludes, "We have started with the Lutheran people, involving them in the planning processes, believing that here lie the answer and strength to overcome the problems and to seize the opportunities of the urban church in this day."

Interdenominational Relationships

At no point in the history of the Christian church and congregational life in America has the door been opened as wide to the congregations participating in interdenominational relationships as today. Dr. Martin E. Niemöller put it well when he stated in Philadelphia a few months ago that "The church's mission cannot be denied by allowing its people to cling to the cozy hearths of their own household gods or by turning their backs and busying themselves in denominational games at a moment in history when the divisions of the beleaguered church militant are crying for the unified command of Jesus Christ to withstand the forces of atheism, skepticism, hatred, and confusion in all areas of the world, in every realm of human life." The ecumenical movement, which is truly one of the miracles of the 20th century, gives us the opportunity to move out boldly, not only across the political and geographical divisions of a divided world, but also across the divisions of the church in all the local places where Christians live and work and witness.

But even beyond this, Karl H. Hertz reminds us, we will still be preaching a kind of "congregational autonomy" if we restrict working together to the Lutheran family. For in many communities we will have only one or two Lutheran congregations. To think that we can go it alone is grossly to underestimate the tasks we are called upon to do, as congregations and as denominations.

Dr. Niemöller voiced two concerns: Christians should not stay behind for safety's sake, and they must not walk their own way, but be led by Christian faith. The essential problem of the church today is not caused by our political-economic differences of conviction; the essential problem, Dr. Niemöller stated, is that few of us on any side are truly willing to recognize Jesus Christ as Lord, even of our economics and politics.

Milwaukee, Wisconsin

A South-Side Inter-Faith Clergy Group has been meeting for the past two and one-half years to deal with the problem and possibility of bringing the mission of the church to bear upon the political and economic community. The 20 Roman Catholic and Protestant clergymen have been studying the South Side with the hope that they could serve the community effectively in terms of spiritual and human renewal and conservation. Their statement of purpose reads, "We believe that the teachings of the church and the principles of our American way of life need to be conserved to have the finest urban culture we can develop for wholesome and strong families and citizens." After numerous conferences with leaders of the Milwaukee community and discussions among the members of the Inter-Faith group, the proposal was made to form a Mitchell Town Community Council. It was recommended that this council be made up of private citizens and representatives of civic groups, churches, businesses, and industries. It would be established in a headquarters office with a full-time director and secretary. Its purpose would be to coordinate the various urban renewal plans and promote conservation redevelopment work where possible.

The association would be financed by residents, businesses, industries, foundations, civic groups, and governments. The reaction to the proposal was favorable to many, but also received considerable opposition. Many did not want to be bothered with the social problems and the problems of urban renewal. It is difficult to rally support until problems become so severe as to be the motivation factor. Aldermen from the area at the public meeting at which this was proposed were very critical, since a council would be another power structure and a threat to their position. The Inter-Faith Council is presently seeking civic groups that would take over the promotion of this project so that it can move on to other ways of improving relations and cooperative efforts among churches.

Cudahy, Wisconsin

Another interfaith group comprising Roman Catholic priests and Protestant pastors in the Milwaukee suburb of Cudahy has recently been formed to attack common problems and further common interests. The organization, called the Clergy Association of Cudahy, is specifically concerned about crime, juvenile delinquency, and pornographic literature. "We do not intend to get into theological debates," the Rev. Stephen G. Mazak of St. John's Lutheran Church, who is president, states. "We respect the differences in each other's beliefs. We will have a chance to study the similarities in pastoral techniques." The group meets once a month in one of the churches and takes a tour of the church after the meeting.

Milwaukee — Lutheran-Roman Catholic Hymn Sing

The second Vatican Council has brought about an entirely new atmosphere in relationship with the Roman Catholic Church. Ascension Lutheran Church in Milwaukee had an opportunity to initiate a new relationship with Holy Ghost Roman Catholic Congregation when last All Saints Day the Lutheran choir, brass ensemble, and organist were invited to the Roman Catholic congregation to assist it in its liturgical renewal. It was indeed a moving experience to see and hear the two congregations sitting together in the pews singing hymns out of the Lutheran hymnal to the glory of God. It was undoubtedly a first in that congregation's history to have "A Mighty Fortress" echoing within its walls. The atmosphere of the entire event was set magnificently by the parish priest, who prayed, "May the Christ of the Ascension send down his Holy Spirit upon us." The path-breaking venture evidenced the fact that even though Christians cannot unite organically, they can unite in the unity of love.

Christian Social Service

Perhaps the best way to begin our faithful journey back to the union in Christ is the one given by Oscar Cullmann, who has suggested that perhaps we should give to each other's poor. Real unity must bear fruit and works of love which are open for all the world to see. This was done in the early church when Paul brought gifts from the churches of Macedonia for the poor in Jerusalem. Christian unity can never be accomplished by merely discussing doctrinal differences nor by seeking for common feelings of fellowship, but if we believe we are really one in Christ despite our differences, we will not hesitate to manifest this faith in works of love to those who are in need among people separated from us.

Milwaukee Good Samaritan Purse

Five years ago at Ascension Lutheran Church in Milwaukee there was developed a small working group within the congregation known as the Good Samaritan's Purse. Its purpose was to assist families within the neighborhood of any background or faith who were in need of material assistance or help. The purpose of the group was to carry out the motif of Jesus' parables and exemplify the new life by having the mind of Christ who was the most loving servant. The five-year record of this faithful dozen in good works is unusual.

The group has taken care of 184 families, averaging one to four families a week for food, never less than six families a week for clothing, and often as many as 12 families a week. In the past five years the group has passed out 73,500 items of clothing, 26,200 items of food, 2,900 pairs of shoes and 300 pairs of boots. In addition to food, clothing, furniture, household articles, utility bills have been paid and fuel has been supplied. Some $8,330 has been collected from church members and $7,693 dispersed. More important, however, has been personal ministry of family to family, assisting in budgeting problems, working out interpersonal relationships within the home and bringing the spirit of Christ into the family. The idea of this local type of congregational project has spread in the past year to 21 other congregations of various denominations and faith, who in turn have evidenced the Christians' concern for one another on the neighborhood congregational level.

Summary

If the world has come of age, then certainly the church must come of age, and this must begin with the local congregation as it examines and relates itself to other congregations in kingdom witness and service. The congregation today, because of the frightening pace of change, has been forced to search its own soul and discover who it really is and whose it is. This is a day of new honesty, new awareness, new mutuality, and new interdependence. The local congregation can no longer specialize in independent action. Both laymen and clergymen need to realize the interdependence of the rural and the urban, the suburban and the inner-city. Selfish introversion, isolation, and competition imply a misunderstanding of the church's ministry and mission.

In all of this God-given newness, both in the opportunities and the problems which it presents, it is impossible for us to look at our church through old glasses or under unchanged categories. As Bishop George L. Cadigan of the Protestant Episcopal Church has stated it, "With newness of God's history, there inevitably and rightly emerge new criteria for estimating the relative health or illness of the church; that is to say, we must measure our effectiveness as a church by asking new questions."

What are some of the new questions which need to be asked on the congregational level?

INTERDEPENDENCE: Does our congregation make practically obvious the dynamic interrelatedness of our congregation with the other congregations in the community?

LAY MINISTRY: Does our congregation take seriously and make visibly efficacious the status of the baptized as priests and servants in the new world? How can individuals catch the excitement once more of their enormous worth as instruments in God's creative work?

ECUMENICITY: Does our congregation consider candidly the divisions in Christendom and work honestly to overcome them in the Spirit of Christ, who said, "Love the brethren"?

TRAINING FOR MISSION: Does our congregation concretely assist us to understand the new world in which we must discover and witness to Christ individually and together as fellow-Christians?

INDIVIDUAL DIFFERENCES: Does our congregation in the inner-city differ from the congregations in the suburbs in the area of attitudes about ourselves and one another?

MUTUAL RESPONSIBILITY: Does our congregation effectively lead us as individual members to outgrow parochialism now? How can our regional and national offices help our congregation work with other congregations of the Lutheran family as well as other Christ-exalting groups?

INWARD RENEWAL: Does our congregation nurture us in patterns of strong worship, honest piety, and winning sanctity appropriate to God's secular age?

MUTUAL INDEBTEDNESS: How can our urban congregation learn to be grateful to the rural church which has prepared the people for the city? How can the suburban church realize its indebtedness to the congregation in the city?

If these questions were taken seriously, a revolution would occur within the church. Or to use a term which is more familiar in our circles, there would indeed be a new reformation, and for each of us a radical renewal. Only as the congregation rediscovers and reexplores its true ministry, will it regain its central driving and overruling sense of mission.

Only as the congregation acquires a "trans-parish" vision will its members be given the sense of being the people of God, new creatures in Christ, and servants of their fellowmen.

13.

Frank P. Zeidler

The Concern for Community

What is the role of the congregation in developing its mission under existing community structures, adjusting to those structures, and influencing their change and improvement? In order to arrive at an appropriate answer to this question it is necessary to carefully examine the meaning and purpose of the community structure.

Definition of Community Structures

Community structures are the existing institutions, physical, social, economic, political, and religious, formal and informal, which dominate the culture of a community. Such institutions may be legal and corporate, such as governments, corporations, educational institutions, and religious bodies; or they may be informal power groupings, such as political clubs. Community structures may be considered also as social institutions and widely accepted community customs, nowhere included in law.

The Purpose of Community Structures

Community structures exist to afford an acceptable means of public and private conduct in meeting the tasks of living for

127

the individual and for the group. Community structures tend to promote the common welfare, to prevent harmful conflict, to resolve differences, and to protect the community from that which the community conceives to threaten it. Community structures also are a means of settling the internal community struggles for scarce economic goods, and for the privileges and power which come with organization of society. Community structures therefore tend to represent the concepts of a people as to that which they consider vital to their social order, and as to the means of delegating power to preserve vital social institutions.

Relationship of the Institution of Government to Private Institutional Structures

For the purposes of discussion, a division is made between those institutions which are private and informal, and those institutions which are formalized through governmental action, such as government itself and laws of government. A constant tension exists between private institutions and other private institutions, and between private institutions and government. This tension arises from the fact that different private institutions and governments have different values about society itself, and each group represented by an institution of some type seeks to extend the value system of the institution ultimately by the formal action of a government. While the common opinion often holds that governments represent a community set of values independent of private institutions and private community structures, the fact is that governments often express the will and values of private institutions and private groups which have gained control of the governmental system by one device or another.

The church as an institution has had many unfortunate experiences with governments in human history, and this experience has crystallized within Lutheran church groups into an institutional principle of church avoidance of governmental authority — the separation of church and state. While at times this principle has produced conditions satisfactory for the church, at other times it has produced an acquiescence to governmental activities which has been exceedingly harmful to church members if not to the formal structure of the church itself.

The Church's Survival Amid Community Structures

From the above reference to the tension between governmental community structures and the church, it can be generalized that the existing community structures can be of such a character that it may be impossible for the church or individual congregations to survive under these structures. An obvious example is control of national governments by despotic individuals; but more subtle conditions arising from economic policies, community policies, social patterns and customs can also militate against the existence of the church. In urban places, as an example, unwholesome forms of recreation, slums, poor social conduct, and bad community values may detract from the ability of an individual congregation to survive and to carry on its mission.

Community Structures with Respect to Needed Community Improvement

Existing community structures can impede needed community improvement and vital social change. The word "structure," applied to community organization, implies the static conditions associated with a physical structure or building. Community life is not static but is undergoing constant change. Community institutions and community structures need to change. The static concept of unalterable permanence in some community structures prevents them from adjusting to new conditions and from providing needed change. If the institutions resist needed change too effectively, society may collapse, or a severe condition of social dysfunction may occur until new institutions evolve.

The attempt to alter community structures which represent

the dominance of a given group in society which is being challenged by another group may produce social disturbance. Thus if the church relates in any way to community structures outside of itself, it faces the necessity of being forced to recognize that it must make some decisions on contending forces which are promoting social change. This is a risk which must be foreseen.

Community Structures and the Mission of the Congregation

It is axiomatic that the individual congregation must be prepared to adjust to community structures and community change just to survive. A congregation cannot be passive to community change, nor can it regard as a matter of governmental concern only institutions and changes promoted by government policy. A congregation ought not always react after the events to community changes which are organized and promoted by some other group. Under such conditions the individual congregation or the church at large can expect that after great changes, a congregation, the church itself, or the leaders, will always be able to associate themselves with a newly emerging power group which has won a struggle to change and to control community institutions. Sometimes the changes in community structure are too hostile to a congregation for it to adjust.

The church, or a congregation, must recognize that there is a constant evolution of community structures and institutions. When it reconciles itself to this fact, it must recognize that a role of the church, and of an individual congregation, is to promote such changes and revisings of community structure as will produce benefits to the community, the individual congregation, and the church itself. In promoting community structural change and improvement, the church must keep in mind the universality of its message and character. If the church in promoting community change has a primary concern for itself, it runs the danger of counterattack from those who feel that the church is challenging their deepest values with only the church's selfish interest in view.

The Church and a Concept of an Idealized Community

To be effective in causing a community structure to evolve to a better state, the church and its individual congregations must develop a concept of an idealized community and a plan to achieve that concept. The concept and plan may be imperfect, but they are usually better than no concept or plan. The new community structure which represents an idealized concept of the church must be rooted in the church's theology and in the church's moral concepts derived from its theology. When the church answers for itself the question of man's relationship to his God and to his fellowman, the development of idealized concepts for community structures is made easier.

The church's concepts of an idealized community must first result in a concept of better social arrangements, and then in the physical arrangements of society to fit those social arrangements. For example, the industrial development of a community may be based not only on the natural resource advantages of the community, but on the moral use of those resources. Machinery for food production may be built instead of armaments, and medicines instead of war gases. Likewise the moral concepts of a church may help determine the quality and kind of housing, the residential pattern, and the physical structures to render community service. Moral concepts may even influence the pattern of community transportation, with a system that favors the disabled, the low income people, and the children.

The Church's Indirect Influence on Change in Community Structures

The church in recent times has had a powerful indirect influence on structural change in American society and in American communities. Housing and social welfare legislation have profoundly affected the social and physical aspect of all American communities. This legislation is the result of the basic moral concepts of the American people which have been derived from religious precepts promulgated by the church. It is also obvious that there are whole sectors of American life where the church has had little influence on socially disruptive factors. The church's basic concept that there is such a thing as moral progression for community life is fundamental to all these changes that have appeared.

The Compulsion on the Individual Congregation to Act

There is a compulsion on the individual congregation to act in the face of changes occurring in community structures. In many cases a congregation will die if it does not act, as in the case of urban decay. A denomination itself will not exist if it does not act in attempting to form new congregations in the changing metropolitan areas. Even the church at large will lose its membership if it does not attempt to bring a relevant message to individual people who are struggling to adjust to the changes forced on their lives by the great changes in society.

The Church's Value as a Shelter for People
Disturbed by Social Change

The considerable changes forced on people in American life today by technology leave many people uprooted and seriously threatened. They have no agency where they can repair for spiritual resource except perhaps the church. Even the home or the extended family cannot provide shelter and comfort for uprooted people. The family usually cannot provide employment for its unemployed members, and in the family there may be no place for the elders or the disabled, as the presence of such people prevents the able members of the family from competing. People may be uprooted from their home communities and lose the mutual support given by neighbors.

A principal role of the church, therefore, must be to provide people with a stable point of reference and with a sense of belonging to a group of people with a common moral framework. The church must give to uprooted or troubled people a sense of support, a role and a purpose to life, and a sense of responsibility to others which can be discharged with satisfactory results. For the mobile community-less people of the nation, the church needs to provide the sense of a community that goes with people wherever they are forced to go by economic and social circumstances.

Church Effort in Practical and Tangible Building of New Structures

To meet the new challenge of the times, the church and individual congregations need to develop new institutions to help people. The church needs more educational institutions in the whole range of education. Practically speaking, this means extension of congregational education efforts. The individual congregations, acting under church guidance, ought to consider developing programs for reaching out into society. New programs for the elderly, the poor, the young, the uneducable ought to be tried by some congregations, and the institutions ought to fit the needs determined by a study of the community to be served. The church and individual congregations must develop more auxiliary institutions.

The Church and New Governmental Efforts to Promote Improved Community Institutions

With new and improved auxiliary organizations and institutions of its own, the church and the individual congregation will be better able to cope with the new conditions created by federal, state, and local governmental efforts, and laws designed to promote community change and alter existing community institutions. This burden will fall with special force on the Lutheran groups who have heretofore shied away from contact with governmental bodies. Such new federal legislation as the elementary and secondary education act, the vocational education act, the economic opportunity act, and the Housing Act of 1965 provide opportunity for congregations to reach out into their communities without suffering the encroachment of government on the domains of religious teaching, and without permitting the church to encroach on the prerogatives of government.

Congregations must also become aware of the efforts of local governments to build community organizations as a means of community improvement. Through these programs congregations or auxiliary bodies of the church can be the media through which public funds can be expended for purposes which are fully consonant with the church's idealized concept of society, thus helping direct the institutional changes which are occurring.

Through auxiliary institutions, or through non-profit institutions organized by church-motivated people, it is now possible to attack the problems of new education, reeducation and training, vocational development, child care and child training, care of the elderly, care of the handicapped, care of the poorly housed, enrichment of the educationally and socially deprived, and many other physical and social problems which distress our society.

Under the various housing acts and provisions, individual congregations in association with other community agencies can now literally remake their own environment. In fact, most obsolete urban environments are likely to be remade under the existing laws within a relatively short time, and the congregation that does not participate in the process will be left out, even to the point of having no building area reserved.

The Probability of Success of the Individual Congregation in Aiding Community Change

There is no guarantee that each and every congregation experiencing the deleterious results of community change can survive. In the case of declining rural areas and central city blighted areas, families may vanish individually to weaken the congregation fatally. However, any congregation, large or small, can exercise some good influence on itself and on its individual members by seeking in some way, however small, to influence the development and improvement of community structures, even if only in its own neighborhood. Those congregational groups which make the best effort to reach out are most likely to survive.

There is, of course, the danger of political reaction to any congregational effort to improve its community and develop its community structures, but this is nothing new in the history of the church itself. The greater danger is inaction in the face of change.

The Congregation's Chance to Grow

By engaging in a conscious effort for community outreach, an individual congregation has a chance to grow in spiritual quality and in numbers. Community outreach will bring congregational members into new contact with other people in the community and extend the influence of the church. This effort is often considered most rewarding by people whose lives have been sheltered from such contact and who do not realize the rich texture of the community surrounding their congregation.

Patterns of Church Outreach

To adjust to the changing community structures, the individual congregation must begin by educating its members to the conditions as they are and to the conditions as they might be. By formal and informal training, individual members should be developed into effective community workers. The congregation itself can participate in community improvement organizations, or encourage its members to form them; and the congregation can provide facilities and aid in developing community programs. Under proper conditions, the individual congregation itself may develop community improvement programs receiving federal, state, or local government assistance. Programs most feasible now are community action programs under the Economic Opportunity Act of 1964 and housing projects under the Housing Act of 1965.

In engaging in programs of community outreach, the congregation must avoid any effort to gain control of government or to influence and control elections. Avoiding these pitfalls, participation by the church in community activities is a desirable activity.

Congregational Influence of Larger Power Structures

The individual congregation can influence the larger power structures of the community by at least three methods. The first of these is by a message from the pulpit. The second is by example of the church in its community activities and outreach and by innovation in social development. The third method is by the activities of individuals whom the church has motivated toward community betterment. In these activities the church and an individual congregation must regard itself as more than a catalyst promoting change without changing itself, but as a spiritual group which is enriching its spiritual life by its expressions in community action.

III.

Congregations in Mission

14.

An Altar in the Alley

Larry F. Gotts

Late on a Thursday afternoon in August, St. Mary Magdalene's Day, a procession makes its way out of the front doors of Grace Lutheran Church, down the cement driveway between the church building and the parish house, headed toward the alley. The processional crucifix and torches which lead the procession are placed in front of a crude table set up there in the alley; the sacramental vessels are placed upon the table-altar, and the celebration of God's greatest gift to the world begins.

As God's people at Grace Church gather at this Eucharistic celebration, now unprotected by the stained glass windows and high walls of the church building, they are dynamically proclaiming to the community that the Word became flesh and dwelt among us — that God so loved the world that he gave his only begotten Son. This God who came in the flesh in a stable at his birth and who died outside the city walls with the refuse of the world, now even today comes to us where we are and where we need him.

Celebration

This service describes the work and mission of Grace congregation. It begins at the altar where God meets us in Christ and

139

unites us in his love, and it processes to the alley where the unloved world lies dying and in need of his love.

Our mission begins at the altar, and thus the worship life of our congregation is central. We gather about the Word and Sacrament weekly, making use of the full liturgical heritage of the Lutheran Church, plus all current liturgical renewal. We begin our work with the involvement of the people in the liturgy, the work of the people. We believe the weekly celebration of the Word of God and the Holy Eucharist is not some gimmick to either get or involve members, but rather the heartbeat and the life blood of God's people. In the first half of the liturgy we hear the Word which calls us to be his people and declares to us our mission, and in the second half we receive the only food that sustains us to be doers of that Word.

It is here at the altar that our people are, first of all, significantly involved. They share not only in the joyful singing of the liturgy but in the reading of the lessons, in the writing and offering of the Prayer of the Church, in the offertory procession, in the exchange of a handshake of Christian friendship at the place of the ancient kiss of peace, and most significantly in the receiving of the Body and Blood of our Lord Jesus Christ. This unites us to Christ and to one another and thus enables us to be his people in this world and to serve as the Body of Christ.

Significant also is the study life of the congregation which involves all ages in both a Sunday church school and an after public school catechism school. Children are enrolled in catechism school as soon as they are enrolled in public school, and they learn how to worship God and serve him as we promised we would teach them when they were baptized.

Compassion

Then we process to the alley. We believe the church is the Body of Christ and thus we must very simply be involved in doing the work of our Lord, be it teaching, preaching, healing, or serving in humble love our neighbor who is in need. As the Body of Christ we must expect to undergo a life experience similar to that of Jesus Christ himself, and we must think of ourselves as being little Christs in our neighborhood, homes, schools, and on the corner where his church building stands.

It means suffering, dying, but it also means the glories of the resurrection. First of all, we are concerned with the youth of our neighborhood, for they are the future and they are those in front of us most crying with tremendous needs. We have the normal Luther League youth, but we are unique in this sense — we have ordinary, violent, antisocial street gangs whom we call our kids too—who are just as welcome and just as much a part of the youth program as the so-called "good kids." If you want to imagine what sort of challenge this type of youth work brings, just imagine what your Luther League would do if you brought a gang into the church. We feel, however, that our youth have grown in their understanding of the mission of the Christian and the church to love the unlovable, and to continue to love and accept and serve people even when they either fail to respond properly to that love or even turn against us.

We believe that social work is a valid and essential part of the mission of the church, for it is love in action. Perhaps the most controversial part of our mission is our cooperation with the neighboring Roman Catholic parish in social work. Here Protestant Community Services and Catholic Youth Organization work hand in hand in dealing with some of the social problems of our neighborhood and its people. Here we believe that Christians across denominational lines have been given a degree of unity to be expressed in this work in our community. The love of Christ is shed forth from both of these parish churches, and we have emphasized not our differences and disagreements but that which we have in common in the Lord Jesus Christ.

This work is not an easy one. It constantly sends us rushing back to the altar. For the alley-without-the-altar is dirty and discouraging. Teen night at Grace Church brings in the hard-to-reach kids off the streets of our neighborhood for recreation and dancing. Sometimes we have 100 or more of these teens together. It is a frightening experience, but bringing them together in some small way expresses the love of the church and her Lord for them, and we are able to get to know them personally and talk with them and understand their needs and problems. There have been some bad times, fights, destruction, bad reputation, and so forth. One night I was standing outside the church on a particularly large teen night when suddenly every light in the church upstairs and down went off. I knew immediately that the main switch had been pulled. I rushed to the side door, entered the church, and pulled back on the main switch just in time to see chairs and tables flying through the air, a social worker hiding behind a post, and the vicar standing in front of me covered with eggs.

The next morning we had much to pray about at the Holy Eucharist. Yes, when your mission is the alley and the unloved and the antisocial and the violent, your need of what happens at the altar is great indeed.

The Servant Way

We suffer and we die, for we are the Body of Christ, and the servant is not greater than his master. My vicar of a year ago made a significant observation. He said that if we had followed a normal and more worldly course in building up our parish, it could have been much richer and larger. We have alienated many people who could not stomach the work with gangs and the rough lower-class elements of our neighborhood. We have lost middle-class Negro members because of our work with lower-class Negroes. We have had to suffer in order to be an integrated church, not only across racial lines but across lines of class and culture. "He eats and drinks with sinners . . ." has been the judgment that the "good" people have made about Grace Church. In order to be faithful to Christ, the church must suffer and die too, taking up its cross. However, there are also resurrections which are worth waiting for, and suffering for, because when we have reached a gang kid with the Gospel and have seen one of the toughest kids of the parish finally confess Jesus Christ as his Lord and Savior and receive Holy Baptism and share with the community in the Eucharist, we have seen a resurrection that no fine building and no "good" reputation can ever provide.

Sometimes we ask ourselves, Are we a success or a failure in our work? We have statistics if headquarters needs them. We reach many, we baptize many, and people are still coming, and worship is well attended, but our work is not justified by statistics, but by the grace and call and command and love of Christ which is shown forth among us. This is all we have to point to. For it is his sacrificial love begun on Calvary which makes possible any real successes and which makes possible the mission of our church—an altar in the alley.

15.

From Tradition

Wallace E. Fisher **to**

Mission[1]

On a crisp November day in 1863 at Gettysburg, Pennsylvania, a tall, gaunt man rose to make a few remarks. The occasion was the dedication of the new national cemetery at Gettysburg. As the sun slipped across Seminary Ridge and poised itself to dip behind the Tuscarora Mountains for the day, Mr. Lincoln, employing three minutes, described the free society more persuasively than anyone has yet managed to do. In the course of these remarks he observed that "the world will little note nor long remember what we say here." The Emancipator, right in so much, was wrong in that judgment. The world knows Gettysburg chiefly because Mr. Lincoln spoke there.

Today, a hundred years later, the writer elects to rip Mr. Lincoln's words out of context and employ them to sum up the critics' judgment on the American parish: the world takes little notice and pays no attention to what is said and done there! One critic, Peter Berger, a professor of sociology at Hartford Theological Seminary, is jarringly blunt:

> The most common delusion . . . is the conviction of ministers that what they preach on Sunday has a direct influence on what their listeners do on Monday. . . . The reality, of course, is that the person listening to the minister in the church is a radically different one from the person who makes economic decisions the next day . . . . In this second life of his the church is totally absent.[2]

144

Gibson Winter argues that the church has fled the central city to live in suburban captivity. The Bishop of Woolwich, Dr. J. A. T. Robinson, argues appealingly, in his little book *Honest to God,* that the church must effect a radical change in its formulation and presentation of Christian truth if it hopes to capture the world's attention. Rudolf Bultmann, convinced that the New Testament is significant only for its essential message, calls for its demythologization, denying its historicity. Dietrich Bonhoeffer at the time of his death appears to have been committed to a non-religious, non-institutional kind of Christianity — "a secular gospel."

Honest Criticism

The twentieth century church does invite criticism. No responsible churchman denies that. The Russian Orthodox Church was an ally of the Czarist suppression of the peasants; the "October Revolution" fell upon it deservedly. Across Europe, the Protestant and Roman churches have been steadily losing touch with the people and today have little more than a tenuous hold on Western Europe. In contrast, the church in America — Protestant and Roman — appears to be a statistical giant in the ecclesiastical record books. But it is a pigmy in the effectiveness of its witness; certainly, it is not God's mighty army.

The critics have a legitimate target in the twentieth century church, and some of their shots hit dead center. The Word of the Lord *is* muted in many corners of the church by "success"-oriented official boards, cautious pastors, and organization-minded ecclesiastics. No clear-cut conviction on the nature and purpose of the church has emerged from the parishes or theological centers.[3] Too often the blind are leading the blind, the bland are counseling the bland, and "perplexed" clergy are following perplexed parishioners. There is talk about "mission" in the institutional centers of the church, but the evidences of a missionary church are spotty. Responsible churchmen, pastors and parishioners alike, know that. Consequently, some are facing up to reality, accepting the demands and promises of Christ, and participating in God's mission to save the world.

Critics Off Center

On the other hand, many critical shots at the church in general and the parish in particular are *not* dead center. The pervasive fear, subtly and openly voiced, that parish renewal is impossible ignores reality and denigrates God's grace. The parish cannot be bypassed. The notion that its billions of dollars in equipment can be scrapped, its vast personnel ignored, and its foundational Book rewritten is nonsense. More significantly, this view doubts God's promise. If one accepts Jesus' word and the apostolic witness, he accepts the called-out, witnessing community as God's idea and handiwork. Unless the clergy believe *that,* they cannot preside over parish renewal.

Further, the clergy who know a bit of church history add perspective to their faith. History testifies that however ineffectual or debased or corrupt the church becomes, it never sinks so low that it cannot produce a remnant. The body of Christ, however weak or maimed, is never a dead body. The Roman church, which fashioned feudalism, did not die with the passing of feudalism. The Orthodox church was wedded to the Czarist state; under the Communist regime it lives uneasily, yet it appears to be healthier today than it has been in centuries. The Methodist revival in eighteenth-century England broke through the formalism of the Anglican establishment, gave a new thrust to Christ's ministry, and moved creatively into the world. "The strange thing about the Church is not that it grows old, but that it seems to have discovered the secret of being born again."[4]

The current disposition to reject the church on the ground that it has not radically improved the social situation must also be examined critically. The church — Roman, Protestant, Orthodox — certainly invites censure for its uncritical allegiance to or passive acceptance of the social *status quo* in many places (the South, suburbia, South Africa) and for its cautious employment of the Word's prophetic utility in the face of political, economic, and social power structures. Those criticisms are relevant, but they must be accepted in the context of the Christian faith. The church — viewed against the biblical image — is seen to exist primarily to save persons through the living Word in preaching and teaching and the sacraments. It is not called out and commissioned to *improve* human nature but to *redeem* it. It does not exist to produce a blueprint for racial justice or to guarantee the success of the United Nations. The church exists to save persons who, worshiping the true God, go out to witness according to their temperament and talent, fashioning the good society *for the sake of the kingdom of God.* The sociological prophets do not carry "chart and compass"; these come from Christ.

The church is the redeemed community, bought with a price, the precious blood of its Lord and Savior Jesus Christ. But it is redeemed for God's purpose: to worship him *in the world* and to witness to him *in the world.* Worship and witness, like love and obedience, are inseparable. Viewed in this biblical context, the church is a secular institution. Those who worship God in Christ are profoundly more worldly than others. They go forth confidently to witness to the victory that Christ has won. They seek to make his lordship known *hic et nunc.* The Methodist lay preachers went into the slums of London. Dibelius went to jail. Bonhoeffer was hanged for plotting to kill Hitler. The worship of God is not a rule of safety.[5] Following Christ, a man gets into the world, and following still, takes up his own cross. Christ's church is notably secular!

In the light of these general observations, let me sketch the course of parish renewal in Trinity Church. There is nothing neat about it! It is essential and existential, objective and subjective; "the wind bloweth where it listeth. . . . "

Faith Needed

First, the pastor must be convinced that parish renewal is possible, that the Gospel is relevant, that Christ enables his church to stand against the gates of hell. We are not calling for a chirping kind of optimism; we are calling for faith *(fiducia),* confidence in God's power to renew his church. If the clergyman is whipped before he begins, renewal will not come in the parish he serves. And if he secretly disdains the parish ministry, the whole church as well as his parish will suffer for its soft-headedness in having ordained him. The Protestant clergy's current preoccupation with their role and the mission of their parish and the need for new forms is getting out of hand. This critical approach, needful and wholesome to a point, *can* become another "church activity" which insulates persons against the reality of God.

Another deterrent to renewal is the egocentric notion among some clergy that they alone face rapid, radical social change in a revolutionary world. Their inability or unwillingness to recognize that political leaders, scientists, educators, business men, and parents are also wrestling with the dynamics of un-precedented social change must constrain the church to examine and assess the emotional resilience and intellectual integrity of its ministerial candidates and veterans.

Parish renewal in urban, suburban, and rural areas *is* possible. Admittedly, there are congregations located so poorly and burdened with a lay leadership so impoverished that renewal is *not* possible. Although Protestant churches presently lack the machinery to do much about parishes of this sort, the parish pastor and his bishop are *free* to say *NO* to church parishes. Unless the pastor is convinced that parish renewal is possible where he serves under the lordship of Christ, his season of leadership there will insulate his people against the reality of God. The last estate of that man and his parish will be worse than the first.

God Has Many Instruments

Second, the responsible parish pastor recognizes that while his parish is intended to be and can be a concrete means through which God works meaningfully in reaching his beloved world in a particular moment of time at a particular place, it is *not* the only means through which God works. The view which sees the parish ministry as the most important ministry for every full-time servant of God is unbiblical, theologically naive, impractical. Equally untrue is the notion that an ecclesiastical official, a board executive, a theological professor, or a campus pastor is a notch or two higher on the "spiritual totem pole" than the "lowly" parish pastor. That some clergy do seek non-parish ministries to escape from the rigors of day-to-day encounters with those who pay their salary, and that some clergy do view non-parish ministries as status symbols are harsh realities in the church. More often, however, this disposition to value one ministry above another stems from theological naivete or ignorance. Actually, authentic persons who exercise Christ's ministry outside the parish know loneliness and criticism and hostility and rejection as sharply as any "prophetic" parish pastor does. Authentic ministry rests on any man's fidelity to the Word in preaching, teaching, dialogue, counseling, and administration wherever the church *calls* him to serve.

As a parish pastor privileged to participate in parish renewal, I have had the support and encouragement of my synodical president, some theological professors, our church executives, and several board secretaries. And Trinity has become involved in and with the "church" beyond its parish boundaries. From the crucible of first-hand experience our lay leaders and clergy have offered several critiques of programs and procedures in the synod and the church-at-large, even as we have supported with mounting vigor the thrusts of the whole church. This give and take between institutional centers of the church and the parishes is an evidence of emotional and intellectual health in both quarters. Indeed, creative tension between the two is an evidence of Gospel faith and love. Actually, each needs the other if Christ's ministry is to be exercised.

A Full Theology

Third, parish renewal calls for the clear-eyed recognition that theological and practical correctives must be viewed only as *correctives,* not as substantive approaches. The current emphasis on "the involved God" (God immanent) dare not obscure the transcendent God. Man and society need him too. The current war on "cheap grace" must not obscure the reality of grace itself. Preaching and teaching the demands of Christ apart from his promises caricature the Gospel. Ethical instruction, separated from the kerygma, may appeal strongly to "social actionists," but it is not the "evangel." And the doctrine of the two kingdoms is still essential to the life of Christ's church.[6]

Then there are the practical correctives. Every alert parish pastor is on guard against the flood of "how to do it" books which imply or suggest that parish renewal can be "had" by some "special" approach or method: (a) Bible study groups, (b) koinonia groups (whatever they might be!), (c) a downtown counseling center, (d) a lay academy, (e) a coffee house, (f) "Gospel preaching," (g) a sound educational program, (h) a jazz liturgy, *ad nauseum*. Any of these approaches can be part of the tactics of parish renewal, but there can be only *one* basic strategy: the hard and existential proclamation of God's Word of judgment and grace. We must be able to say, *"Thus says the Lord."*

Further, "the parish viewed as a mission field" must not lead to another false thrust — namely, that one works at converting "church members" for ten years and then sends them "outside" into the world. The responsible clergyman and his lay leaders work in the parish and in the world at the same time. The parish church is viewed properly as the center of worship and learning and pastoral care where the Word motivates and equips clergy and laity alike to go immediately into the world to witness, however falteringly; to test the doctrine for themselves; to say a good word — albeit ineptly — for Jesus Christ. At Trinity we engaged so messily in both at the same time that with the perspective of a decade I cannot identify precisely where one ended and the other began. Specifically, the clergy and a few laymen accepted immediately the view that unless we spoke for God in and to the world, no matter how inadequately, God's Word might not be spoken in the place where he had set us. The love of Christ constrained us to speak to and get inside the power structures of our community, to shape public opinion wherever we could.

The commotion and tension and conflict engendered by this conviction — boldly acted on — are indescribably severe in our religionized culture. But out of Trinity's experience we can and do testify that even as the servant of Jesus Christ is in the process of maturing, even as he struggles to articulate his faith, even as he works to grow under the judgment and grace of God, he can effectively bear witness to the lordship of Jesus Christ. If the person is authentic and the message is God's, the messenger makes an impact on the world.[7]

Awareness

Fourth, both clergy and laity must recognize, identify, and face up to the need for renewal in their congregation. It is easier for most of us to discuss parish renewal at a conference or retreat than it is to face squarely the need for it in one's own parish. Facing it there requires painstaking study, careful listening to the membership and the community, and the concrete identification from the pulpit and in every corner of the parish of the areas of need. This hard, exhausting process of diagnosis, identification, confrontation, and rugged correction rests on the commitment, biblical faith, theological knowledge, emotional resilience, and skills of the clergy *and* lay leaders.

At Trinity, parish renewal began at the top. That, in my judgment, is crucial.[8] The parish leaders accepted their responsibility to do and to be, by God's grace, what the Gospel requires of every Christian. The tensions and conflicts engendered among us in those early years of encounter with the Word brought pain before healing and new life came. From there — and at the same time — the renewal process moved slowly throughout the parish and immediately into the world, gaining an uneven momentum across the years.

Painstakingly, we identified the images nurtured and projected by Trinity. The congregation's image in the synod was lack-luster: it had not met its apportionment during the preceding two years and had refused to discuss its part in realigning synodical boundaries. Trinity's image in the community was even less attractive: a proper, proud, exclusive congregation, a firm bulwark against social change in which it was *not* involved. Several congregational self-images were equally hurtful. (1) The congregation expected recognition and respect in Lancaster and in Lutheran circles. The "old guard" attitude was hard as nails: "the building is sacred; Muhlenberg's constitution (1769) is sacred; the practices and traditions of the church are superior to those in any other church. Touch nothing, disturb nothing, change nothing."[9] (2) The lay leaders recognized that worship attendances were minimal, budgets unrealistic, the church school faltering, the congregation uninvolved with the community, but neither the vestry nor the pastor had any notion then (1952) of the tensions and searing conflicts which would be the prelude to the rebirth of ministry in Trinity parish. (3) The parish expected its clergy and vestry to solve its problems; the parishioners were outside the life and work of the congregation.

"The primary need was for the clergy, vestry, and the parish to come under the Word of the Lord in judgment and grace so that the Holy Spirit could call and persuade persons, each deciding for himself whether he would take up Christ's ministry. The birth of corporate ministry was the only road to the congregation's recovery of God's mission, its only chance to survive. Trinity had to decide."[10]

Community Knowledge

Fifth, if parish renewal requires that the clerical and lay leaders identify and face up to the images projected by the congregation, it also requires that they examine critically the community in which the congregation exists. "Old Lancaster," the oldest inland city in the United States, sustained "Old Trinity," the oldest church in the oldest inland city. "Social changes in the community of Lancaster, in spite of galloping industrial and urban expansion, were reluctant, grudging, slow of pace in 1953. The Lancastrian, his antecedents deep in Colonial history and Pennsylvania Dutch culture, is not disposed to change; his propensity for order often throttles the dynamics for social and economic justice. The stately dowager (Trinity) identified herself easily with this powerful, pervasive cultural *status quo*. Naturally, those people least disposed to pioneer felt most comfortable in her own company."[11]

This conformity to the community had to be broken if Trinity was to exercise Christ's ministry in the world. At the same time, "pious" Trinity had to learn to listen to the world, to dialogue, in order to preach the Word relevantly and to teach it effectively. The key words in this continuing experience of renewal are freedom, confrontation, conflict, suffering, crucifixion. There is no easy path to parish renewal.

Ministry of the Word

Sixth, parish renewal requires the pulpit, the classroom, and the counseling hour. The proclamation of the Gospel motivates persons to repent and believe in Christ. Evangelical teaching equips them to serve Christ in the parish and in the world. Pastoral counseling brings the resources of the Word to bear on particular areas of personal inadequacy, enabling persons to love persons. Koinonia results. "A real sense of Christian vocation emerges among the laity, when, viewed as subjects rather than objects, they are confronted with the Word in their freedom and equipped and enabled from it to witness and serve."[12]

Form Is Essential

Seventh, institutional forms are inescapable. Man is not a disembodied spirit. He depends upon and devises institutional forms (family, government, church, school) to communicate spirit and truth, to share love, to fashion order, and to establish justice. God himself had to employ men and events and finally to incarnate himself in the Man from Nazareth to communicate intelligibly with man. In Jesus, God met man "eyeball to eyeball." "Christ's Church is the historical means through which he continues to confront persons in time. From the beginning it fashioned evangelical forms to embrace and care for persons in its community, preserve apostolic truth, and carry the Gospel into the world. Christianity has been able to bridge the centuries by providing a Spirit-inhabited institution through which the Word could become flesh in every generation. These institutional forms must be examined continuously to determine whether they are means or ends, but institutional means are inescapable."[13] Dynamic conservation and responsible innovation are strands in the continuing renewal of the church. Change for the sake of change is not the way to renewal.

No form, old or new, is relevant unless it communicates the living Word to persons so that they can decide *for* or *against* Christ. The new wine of the Gospel is the church's primary need. But the born-again parish does not disdain institutional forms. A Spirit-filled ministry, lacking structure and order, must dissipate its force. The Holy Spirit, seeking to persuade persons in their freedom to follow Christ, is helped or hindered by institutional forms. The born-again parish constantly brings them under the constant scrutiny of the Word so that they may help rather than hinder. It seeks to fashion a flexible structure in which continuing renewal can occur.

Authentic Image

Finally — "because the image of ministry entertained and projected by pastors and people affects radically the degree to which the church exercises Christ's ministry, it is imperative that both discern and orient to an authentic image. The quest for this image begins not within the context of the profession, but within the context of the faith. Standing humbly before the tribunal of biblical evidence, one discovers that the authentic minister begins as a man — perverse, finite, lost — justified through faith, made new in Christ, but still a man. The Holy Spirit uses this new creature, obedient in his freedom, to communicate the living Word through his freedom. This shepherd-prophet, grateful that he is cared for by Christ, cares for others from Christ's love, confronting them with Christ's demands and promises, and equipping them from the Word to be prophets, teachers, and evangelists.

"The authority which prompts this confrontation is not resident in an order, a dogma, or a liturgy; it is in the living Word. Ministry, dogma, and liturgy carry God's authority only when they testify to Christ. No servant of the Word, therefore, directs, manages, or manipulates persons; he knows that the Holy Spirit declines these activities and that the human spirit, although seeming at times to respond to them, cannot escape the implications of human freedom without perverting its essential nature.

"Parish renewal is not likely to happen apart from parish pastors who, disciplined in their daily dependence on God to handle the responsibilities of shepherding, are also theologically knowledgeable, emotionally resilient, and intellectually curious. It is unrealistic to assume that the clergy need expect nothing of themselves in leadership which laymen do not expect from themselves. Shepherding is preeminently the ordained minister's task."[14]

"It is a perversion of the concept of the priesthood of believers to allow Christ's ministry to rest wholly on the ordained minister and a few parish leaders. . . . it is an equally unrealistic reading of that concept to assume that the laity are waiting eagerly in the wings to witness and render priestly service. They need to be motivated, enlightened, equipped, and encouraged from the resources of God's Word (1 Peter 5:1-4). They need a script, a producer, a prompter, a 'lead actor.' Shepherding is preeminently, but not exclusively, the ordained minister's task. Luther put it tersely: 'We are all priests, but we are not all clergymen.' "[15]

Conclusion

Parish renewal "may seem insignificant in a nation where people rush wildly one year to build fallout shelters, stand eyeball to eyeball with their adversary the next, and boast the following year that they will be the first to place a man on the moon. But to see how God uses one church to save some people from self-destruction is to see how he can use his church to save the world from annihilation. Salvation is not only eschatalogical; it is mundane."[16]

Footnotes

1. Wallace E. Fisher, *From Tradition to Mission* (Nashville: Abingdon Press, 1965).
2. Peter L. Berger, *The Noise of Solemn Assemblies* (Garden City: Doubleday & Company, 1961), p. 37.
3. H. Richard Niebuhr, *The Purpose of the Church and Its Ministry* (New York: Harper & Row, 1956), pp. 17-18.
4. Daniel T. Jenkins, *The Strangeness of the Church* (Garden City: Doubleday & Company, 1955), p. 14.
5. This thought, as I recall, was first expressed in this fashion by A. N. Whitehead.
6. Gerhard Ebeling, *Word and Faith* (Philadelphia: Fortress Press, 1963), pp. 386-406, presents "the necessity" for the doctrine. Harvey Cox, *The Secular City* (New York: Macmillan Company, 1965), pp. 107-108, presents a critique of the doctrine.
7. Fisher, *op. cit.* chapters 3 and 5.
8. *Ibid.*, pp. 169-175.
9. *Ibid.*, p. 30.
10. *Ibid.*, pp. 28-35.
11. *Ibid.*, p. 26.
12. *Ibid.*, chapter 6.
13. *Ibid.*, chapter 7.
14. *Ibid.*, pp. 184, 185.
15. *Ibid.*, pp. 46-47.
16. *Ibid.*, p. 187.

16.

Paul Biegner

Witness in
an Agricultural
Service Center

Thief River Falls is a city of nearly 7,500 people located in northwestern Minnesota, approximately 300 miles north of Minneapolis-St. Paul. It is an over-churched city which has 17 resident clergy serving fourteen churches, ranging from six Lutheran congregations of various backgrounds, to a wide spectrum of Protestant groups, and the Roman Catholic Church.

The city owes its beginning to the rivers which flow through it, and also to wheat. The rivers are important as the center of a system of regional and community parks which offer swimming, water skiing, camping, and picnicking facilities. However, before the turn of the 20th century, wheat that was grown in the valley had to be hauled by oxcart to nearby mills for processing into flour. Water was the only source of power, which made location on a river necessary. Thus, in the mid-1880's a flour mill and dam were built on the river and Thief River Falls was born. The small flour milling settlement grew considerably when the area was opened up for timbering. Again the river played a major role by providing power for the saw mill and by serving as a means of floating the logs from cutting areas to the mill. The lumber industry caused the population to increase from only 191 residents in 1890 to a population ten times its size by the turn of the century. An even greater spurt of growth was experienced in the decade between 1900 and 1910. The town was named rail center for the Soo Line's Winnipeg division, which, coupled with the opening of eleven townships of Indian reservation land for homestead farming, accounted for a growth to a population of over 2,700 by 1910. When timber became depleted, the saw milling industry died. Fortunately, Thief River Falls is near the east edge of the Red River Valley of Minnesota and North Dakota, which makes it well suited for raising small grains, flax, and potatoes, as well as for the operation of diversified dairy and beef farms. As a result, the city grew around agriculturally oriented enterprises such as grain elevators and dairies which served an extensive surrounding area. The city's excellent rail facilities contributed much to its growth as a regional center. With a strong agricultural base, the city grew to be a prime trade and service center in far northwestern Minnesota.

Within the ferment of taming the far northwestern frontier, St. John Church had its first beginning some 70 years ago. As early as 1888 services were held by a German-speaking pastor in the homes of a handful of German settlers. In 1895, one year before Thief River Falls was incorporated, St. John congregation was organized. Thus St. John Church took its place as one of eleven churches in the midst of 23 saloons in that rough-and-tumble lumberjack town.

Factors Limiting Growth

From the beginning the growth of St. John Church was hampered by several factors.

There were relatively few Germans in the late waves of settlers and homesteaders, which resulted in a small base for membership. Most arrivals were Norwegian immigrants, with a mixture of Swedes and French from Canada. The Germans settled as small and scattered islands in a vast sea of Norwegians.

To serve these isolated pockets of German settlers was a large task. Pastoral manpower was often stretched nearly to the breaking point. In the years before World War I, St. John's missionary-pastor also served up to 13 congregations and preaching stations for nearly 13 years. On Sundays a circuit of more than 70 miles was made with buggy or sled and team of bronchos to serve three of the six stronger congregations. On four or five days of the week the pastor rode the trains north and south, east and west, to serve preaching stations and small congregations in other towns as far as 75 to 100 miles away. Poor and often nonexistent roads further complicated travel so that St. John had Sunday services only every third week for some time.

Because of the city's geographic isolation, and because of the strong prohibitionist feeling among many of the people, private clubs and lodges have been extremely popular. The Masons, Elks, Odd Fellows, and Eagles all have strong representation. The Eagles lodge alone has more than 1,500 active members. The membership base was further constricted because of the congregation's strong stand against membership in fraternal organizations and lodges.

Over the years the congregation's stance became rather defensive and tainted with a strong sense of inferiority. Most of the merchants, teachers, and professional people have belonged to the Methodist or other Lutheran parishes. The other mainline Lutheran churches were and are considerably larger than St. John's 340 communing and 575 baptized members. By an inverse sort of pride, some felt that being smaller was a sign of being a pure and true "little flock." Throughout St. John's history the congregation has been on the outside looking in. A symbol of this has been the location of the parish's buildings. The first two buildings of the congregation were right on the edge of town fronting on a large swamp. The new A-frame building constructed in 1958 was also erected on the very edge of town, away from the heart of the community, its thought and its action. St. John Church has had a tendency to see itself as a smaller and less successful competitor of the other Lutheran parishes. As a result it has looked to the other congregations for its signals, taking its signals from Trinity Church rather than from the divine Trinity's instruction in Holy Scripture.

Underlying Principles for Mission

Basic to the task of renewal in St. John Church and a revital-
ization of its mission are the assumptions and principles which
are more thoroughly discussed in the paragraphs which follow.

The church is the product of God's justification. What God
calls the church to be by his justifying verdict the church actually
is. In Christ God reached out to a lost and sinful world. His outreach became visible in an infant's crib, a carpenter's sweat, a
helper's healing hand, a criminal's cross, and a conqueror's
boulder-burst grave open forever. God's justifying verdict ren-
dered at the cross and open grave is effective for any and all
who will believe it. That verdict is not merely empty words, but
calls the church into existence and bestows a new condition.
What God calls us to be we *are*. The church and its mission are
a present reality in Christ, not some distant ideal or future goal,
though their ultimate goal lies in God's end. The total activity
of the church has as its target that of all members in Christ
becoming what they are in Christ.

Christ's Mission

The mission of Jesus Christ to the world shapes the mission
of the church to the world. Jesus Christ is the one constant and
determinant in the Christian church's mission. Christ did not
serve himself; he did not manipulate or pull rank. He served
among men who were free to manipulate him, use and abuse
him, and in their cold rejection sent him to the cross. Hence,
God glorified him at the resurrection and ascension, giving him
lordship over the universe. Similarly, the church exists not by
self-assertion — certainly not by continually affirming and justifying itself — but by the self-less ministry of Christ to the world.
The Servant-Church demands no special prerogatives, pulls no
special rank, but presents the Gospel and pursues its mission to
the world in the name of the Lord. Only by being world-centered
in the same way the divine Servant was, can the church really
be the church. Being church-centered, regarding the church as

a safe refuge from the world, is a betrayal of its calling to be the servant people of the suffering Servant. Only by not being and not *wanting* to be an end in itself does the church arrive at being the church.[1]

The whole church is God's missionary force to the world. Summoned by Christ, they are sent to the world and into the world, just as Jesus Christ was sent to and into the world. They are the body of which Christ is the controlling head. We are not thinking of an elite or a select laity, but the laity as it is. The determining factor is that people are in the domain of Christ and his Spirit. To systematically treat lay people as immature keeps them immature. Conversely, to treat them as mature, spirited people and to give them responsibility and avenues of service and expression is to help them mature.

The church's mission must be sacredly secular, always world-centered not church-centered. The servant-church exists for the world's sake. The church is not God's end goal, the world is. "God so loved the *world* that he gave his only begotten Son." "God was in Christ reconciling the *world* to himself . . . and has committed to us the word of reconciliation."

The Enabler

The pastor should see his ministry primarily as enabler — an equipper of God's people. He serves as playing coach — not the whole team. He recruits, trains, and fortifies God's people for their task of being God's team in every place, at every time. Or, taking another analogy, he is like a skilled chemist, combining Word and people under the catalyst of the Spirit's power, for potent faith and new products of mission and ministry to God's world.

At St. John Church we try to keep the above basic principles of the nature of the church and its mission foremost. The church council spends a considerable amount of time at each of its

---

[1]Hendrik Kraemer, *A Theology of the Laity* (Philadelphia: Westminster Press, 1959, p. 130.

monthly meetings in a constant review and analysis of the parish, its mission, and its structure in the light of these principles, and in the light of the challenges of the community and God's world. As a thoughtful task force the church council keeps asking, (1) What is the mission of the church and what are the specific tasks and challenges of this parish toward that mission? (2) How is what we are doing meeting the unique challenges of God's world in this place? (3) How is what we are doing bringing about a changed people under the Spirit?

Vital Worship

One place where we have begun at St. John Church is in the area of worship. The justifying verdict of God calls his church into existence, and it is around that justifying verdict in Word and Sacrament that the church gathers. Here we have much to learn from the Book of Acts. The early church was a living fellowship that had a soul-shaking experience of Jesus Christ. When he was torn from their midst by the cross and restored to life, the disciples were certain he was God. He was present as unseen Host at their joyous celebrations of the Lord's Supper. They couldn't forget him. All of the apostles' preaching constantly struck the emphasis of the once-crucified, but everliving Lord.

Our dreary trouble is that all too few are really aware of the ever-present living Christ. Too often the keynote in our congregational worship has been the real absence of Jesus Christ, rather than his real presence. Renewal has started with our worship services, where the Spirit of the risen Christ speaks to us in his Word, and the risen Lord gives us his body and blood in the Sacrament. Again and again we patiently teach and instruct the parish about the meaning, method, and experience of worshiping together. We have tried to help our people understand that Christians best serve one another when we serve each other the Word. To that end in place of the Introit we have restored Psalms prayed by the entire congregation. The elders of the parish occasionally read Scripture lessons and as representatives of the entire people of God always assist at celebrations of the Lord's Supper.

We saw the need to stamp out the spectator mentality in our parish's worship. So we provided for thoughtful variation in the liturgy. On occasion we sing hymn settings of the creed, Christmas hymns replace the Gloria in Excelsis, or an Easter or Ascension hymn is sung in place of the Gradual. Also litanies are composed for special occasions such as when students leave for college, Labor Day and national holidays. A variety of general prayers are used and often prayed antiphonally. We accent our praise of God by having the congregation rise for hymn verses which are doxological in character. Above all we feel that if worship is the celebration of the real presence of Jesus Christ in Word and Sacrament then we cannot tolerate being cold, lazy or half-hearted and downright sloppy in our worship and response to his Word. To give splendor to our worship, we use the limited gifts that we do have available. Choirs sing regularly and brass choirs occasionally play preludes and voluntaries for festival days. Church attendance has improved 20% over the 1963 figure, though membership has remained stable. Constantly we stress that God's people gather around the forgiving Word for cleansing only to be scattered back into daily life. We withdraw from the world to return to the world. When Christ is acknowledged as the Lord to be served in all life, then appetites are sharpened for his grace shared in worship. Where there is little awareness of being Christ's pilgrim people on the march, even the food for the march, Word and Sacrament, tastes stale and dull.

Beyond Isolation

Because the church is the product of God's justification, parish leaders and pastor felt we must take ecumenical matters out of the realm of the sanctified optional and place them squarely within the necessary and essential part of our mission. Despite past isolation, we felt that we would have to start talking with our fellow Lutherans and then start working with them. We came to the conclusion that we were one church — the Lutheran Church at work in the Thief River Falls area, and not three separate church bodies with three separate Gospels and three separate missions. We may have very serious differences in the area of lodgery and fraternal organizations, but God's Spirit has called us to assist one another in mutual growth, study, and work wherever possible.

We were convinced in principle that competition is not good for the church, as it is for business. Rivalry and competition among our Lutheran parishes in Thief River Falls does not keep us on our toes as much as it keeps us on one another's toes; it hurt far more than it helped. Accordingly, when Thief River Falls was chosen as the site of the state junior college, St. John's church council had already long before concluded that we would not attempt any separate work among the 350 students at the area vocational school and junior college. Rather we initiated a proposal that all four mainline Lutheran churches work together and not in a competitive fashion. The St. John church council's proposal to combine efforts and programming and to share staff, equipment, and buildings was received enthusiastically. We hope that this beginning can be merely the start for continued cooperation in joint study and common strategy for Lutherans in the Thief River Falls area.

Building in Love

The church builds itself in love. Mutual nurture through rich intake of the Word is needed so that the parish may be about its mission in God's strength. At St. John Church we aim at a minimum of three spiritual visits to each member family in the parish during a year. House-to-house visitation, cottage meetings, and group meetings at the church are the familiar techniques used. The Board of Elders heads up an annual visitation on matters such as how to read the Bible, how to conduct family devotions, how to pray. The Stewardship Committee aims its visit not primarily for the solicitation of funds and pledges, but above all for telling the story of God's grace and the church's mission. The pastor has a planned pastoral visiting program in which every household of the parish is reached every year or year and a half. Appointments are made at least a week ahead of time by telephone or when people come to announce for Holy Communion. A letter explaining the specific purpose of the visit and a brochure or outline to study in advance are enclosed in a mailing to the family when the appointment is made. Thus the entire household is present and prepared for the visit. Part of the hour and a half visit is slotted for a Bible discussion from the outline already provided in advance. Questionnaires, check lists, and question and answer periods stimulate discussion and participation. The entire visit is kept on a warm, informal basis.

In addition, the congregation sponsors evenings with the Pastor for small groups of 20 to 25. These groups are mixed from various areas of the parish so that people get to know one another as they bend elbows in a coffee hour that follows. For an hour and a half the pastor through joint worship, films, Bible study, and lecture can concentrate on one major emphasis. Such an evening recently encouraged attendance at the Lord's Supper with the small and large Catechisms serving as the focus. Evenings with the Pastor are structured for basic fellowship outside the auxiliary organizations and permit the Pastor to inform, inspire, and sensitize.

The Whole Church Is God's Missionary Force to the World

At St. John Church our underlying assumption has been that lay people are not to be viewed as the helpless, uninformed, and ignorant, but "as that part of the church that has to carry the brunt of the burden of encounter with the world in and around themselves."[2] Further, we have assumed that preparation for evangelism is to preach the Gospel. Where the Gospel has been proclaimed, the only further way to get ready for evangelism is the work of evangelism. We must expect fruitful outreach by the

---

[2]Kraemer, *op. cit.,* p. 114.

laity as an outcome of fruitful faith. The mission of the Savior makes missionaries for the Savior; the Evangel makes evangelists.

Lay Evangelism

Quite frankly, an aggressive program of outreach is a must. Most new arrivals in the city come from the solidly ALC strength of northern Minnesota. Nearly all of them transfer to the two large ALC churches, and we do not attempt to divert them into St. John Church. So, much of our outreach is to the dechurched and unreached or unreachable. Nor is Thief River Falls in the line of growth. Thief River Falls, along with most of northwestern Minnesota, lost more residents from population movement than were gained, and most of the loss came in the ages of 20-40 among child-bearing families. A recent projection has indicated that Thief River Falls will show slight growth of population to perhaps 8,500 by 1980. The city's isolation means that there will be little economic growth or stimulation from a metropolitan center. Prospects are constantly gathered and systematically cultivated. The Welcome Wagon and power company prospects are followed up carefully. The congregation has in-church surveys two or three times a year. The pastor spends one afternoon a week in the hospital visiting those who indicate they are unchurched, Lutheran, or Protestant, but list no parish pastor.

The pastor asks the nearest member to pay a friendly first call to any new prospect in the name of St. John Church. The woman may bake a batch of cookies or a loaf of bread and the couple talks in a warm and enthusiastic way about their parish and informs the prospect that the pastor will be coming. This is by way of pre-evangelistic contact. A ladies' aid calling group is trained to explicitly tell the Good News. The congregation also has an ambassador's calling emphasis every two months during the winter, fall, and spring in which volunteers are trained for witness. In addition, the pastor aims at making a minimum of 10 evangelistic calls every week that he is in town. All prospects are cultivated through the mails. A monthly parish newsletter, letters with tracts and letters urging them to view "This is the Life" in their homes, keeps before prospects the message which St. John Church bears.

Ministers in Society

In the public domain the real uninterrupted contact between the church and the world happens through the laity. All members of the church are God's missionary force every day as they are dispersed into the world. In the office, store, and machine shop, in the political party, in the NFO, Farm Bureau, or Farmers' Union, in the courthouse, welfare agency, or club, in the school, in the radio station, or home where sacred and secular meet, where vital decisions are made and enacted, the layman is to be the church. Here is where the pastor's ministry at St. John takes a decidedly servant form. The witness and service of the laity to the world cannot be done by the pastor. He is not there. He does not have these contacts in sufficient measure. The pastor's task is to be a servant to the servants of God.

For the pastor's role of assistant layman we have employed small groups in our parish. At St. John the pastor honeycombs the parish with small groups meeting once a week. Two or three a week are set up, whenever possible. A considerable amount of time is spent teaching the laity to be the church, to do constantly in the neighborhood what the pastor can do only sporadically — something they can do, often more effectively. What it means to belong to Jesus Christ and to be a member of his church is the main content. The pastor's first obligation is to minister to those who are already Christians, so that they may become a serving and saving community in the world.

The *koinonia* of these small groups is built around study of the Bible, prayer, and training in witness, stewardship, and Christian behavior and action. All respond to Scripture; by intercession each supports the other's witness and service; all are trained, equipped, and stirred by the living proclamation of the Word by each and by all. Until now there has been no celebration of the Lord's Supper in these "house-churches," but that expression of the *koinonia* may be a future development.

Two or three groups a week are set up, when possible. These study groups rotate around the parish. The farm families meet in the late fall and winter: one group 15 miles east and north, another group 10 miles east and south and another 5-10 miles to the south and west of the city. Several small groups also meet in different areas of the city and in adjoining trailer courts — spring, summer, and early fall when field work is in full swing. These are usually short-term study groups meeting for about two months in one place, then moving on. Every eligible member family in the area receives a letter and tract on Bible study from the pastor. Prospects from the immediate area are also invited for exposure to the Word as studied and lived. Information about the Bible study group also is shared by two women appointed as hostesses for each area who recruit and remind by telephone.

Small groups are sometimes formed as vocational fellowships, equipping Christians to meet a rural environment that increasingly seems to take it for granted that God is beside the point. Farmers and factory workers wrestle with the pressures of a big machine economy with technical help. Parents study family life. All gain insight through group sharing on today's problems in the light of Scripture.

In small group work the pastor must be a good listener and willing learner. For example, there are acute frustrations built into any lay confrontation of the public domain. After all, the church is no longer on center stage. It has no real claim on control, except through the supple and limber involvement of the laity. The basic question is: "Where in our technocracy are the centers of power to be found?" It is not just that the church no longer controls the big leaders, but that even the big leaders no longer control the centers of power. Just try to find the centers of power in either city or small town. Where are they — in government, business, banking, cooperatives, or labor? Once in a fairly uninvolved society Nathan could face David, and Jeremiah could confront Jekoiakim through his scribe. Today the question is: "Where's the king?" So the pastor learns from his people, seeks information, asks patient questions, and listens as the church reports as the Spirit has blessed their witness and service.

One other expression of our parish's *koinonia* could be mentioned — our circles of intercession. When the pastor learns of some crisis in the parish, such as an illness, a death, or some other need for prayer and personal support, he phones the chairman of the Ladies' Aid, who in turn notifies leaders of the Ladies' Aid circles, who in turn notify the rest of the parish of the need for prayer or assistance. Recently a young family of St. John lost everything in a tornado; two days later a door collection of several hundred dollars was gathered, boxes of clothing for adults and children were contributed, and a kitchen shower was held a day or two later.

Conclusions

1. At St. John Church renewal begins by believing the Gospel. Because the Good News is good and Christ is Lord, we optimistically face our task of ongoing renewal. We assume optimistically that the whole church is the people of God, God's servant-church and missionary force to the world. So we have not felt compelled to abandon the leaking and floundering ship of the parish church.

2. Rather, we have worked for a growing core of the committed, who know who they are and whose they are. We have started with our common worship. A system of at least three visits a year to every household in the parish by elders, pastor, and stewardship committee is another step in this direction. Small groups formed around the *koinonia* of Bible study, prayer, and training are aimed at developing and expanding a growing number of "quiet fanatics" for Christ.

3. Though numerically still a tiny island of Missouri in the midst of an ALC sea, we feel we must work for as wide an amount of joint study, cooperation, and coordination as possible. Ideally, we look forward to one Lutheran strategy for our area.

4. We continue to look for change that is rapid and ongoing. We dare not merely be open for business as usual, for what was once right and true can later be false, irrelevant, and even immoral. Through continuing analysis we are going to try to be more world-centered, less church-centered. As God's Spirit blesses we will pray and work that our mission to our segment of the world may be more closely conformed to that for which God sent his Son — that the *world* might be saved through him.

17.

Robert A. Onkka

Merged for Mission to the Countryside

There are two critical issues facing the parish I serve — and facing every parish: to be relevant and to have something to say. I should simply like to report, with some understanding, our mission to be relevant to our day and our place.

On January 1, 1961, three congregations in and around the small village of Valders, Wisconsin, merged to form a single congregation of 1,000 members and took the new name of Faith Lutheran Church. On August 30, 1964, their new $400,000 sanctuary and Sunday school unit was dedicated. The outstanding architecture of the church has brought a great deal of publicity. Soon after its dedication a Green Bay television station had a 5-minute feature telecast on the building. The Manitowoc *Herald Times*, a daily paper in our city 12 miles east of Valders, had two full-page spreads: one on the usual coverage of the dedication of a new church, the other featuring the architecture and sculptures. The Sunday *Milwaukee Journal* ran a feature article on the church from the standpoint of the impact it has made in the community. *The Lutheran Standard* featured on its cover and two interior pages the symbolism of the church and its sculptures. In the past year over 7,000 visitors have toured the church. During the first few months there were so many visitors that the congregation arranged for "church sitters" to be there during daylight hours and to conduct tours around the building. Art classes from two nearby colleges and two nearby large high schools have studied the church. Sunday school classes, vacation Bible schools, and many other groups have made special trips to study the symbolism of the church. In an area where the population is 47% Roman Catholic, a new bond of understanding has arisen. Over 400 Roman Catholic nuns have toured the church, many of whom have said, "This is the first time I have ever been in a church not of my own faith." Rarely a day passes without tourists traveling by on busy Highway 151 stopping in and saying, "We just had to stop."

All of this in a village of 622 people!

The reaction of the congregation to the new building has been a phenomenal acceptance of its striking, modern architecture. There was some fear that our older members would not feel at home. This has not been so. A case in point concerns one of our older members who has just celebrated her 90th birthday. She was being driven past her old church, which is now being torn down. Her daughter feared what she would say when she saw the old church going down. She said simply, "They're tearing down Gjerpen. That's too bad. But the new church is nice."

Attendance has shown a marked increase with about 10% more members attending church now than before. With special consideration for the aged and infirm, we have several coming to church now who hadn't been at services for years. In fact, one Sunday one member who had been quite opposed to the idea of the new church came for the first time. While he was taking off his coat and getting ready to enter the sanctuary, he saw two people coming in wheel chairs — he watched with understanding. He's been an avid supporter ever since.

Our community has appreciated our church. It is quite typical in Wisconsin for community activities such as the county homemakers to meet in the public halls attached to taverns, as there is really no other place to meet. We have found our church being used more and more for such activities and we welcome them without charge to use our facilities.

Reasons for Merger and Building

There were many who asked, "Why build a new church?" At the time of the merger the two country congregations had baptized memberships of 479 and 289, while the church in the village had 336. These were not small, struggling congregations which had to merge to survive. They could have continued as they were for another 100 years. But the reasons for the merger and the building of the new church seemed to be primarily five in number.

A stronger program of worship and teaching in the congregation. Let's face it — there often isn't much about these "pretty little country churches" to encourage an active and meaningful church program unless the size of the congregation is in keeping with the size of the building.

A stronger witness of the congregation to the community. How do you explain to an unchurched family three churches of the same faith and the same synod — the farthest three miles from Valders, the other only one mile? How do you explain the need for Christ and his church in such a situation? Related to this is the fact that with 47% of the population Roman Catholic, there are a tremendous number of mixed marriages, and we were losing more than our share, primarily because we seem unimportant.

A more efficient structure. The demands on the pastor's time and the maintenance on three old and inadequate buildings were too high a price to pay.

A practical necessity. There were inadequate Sunday school facilities in all three buildings, but this was felt most acutely by the village church which was experiencing a slow but steady growth. They were of the growing conviction that something must be done immediately or they would do it alone. The District President called special meetings of the congregations — but to no avail. The open country churches constantly voted "No." During this time the pastor resigned and the Call Committee spent a futile nine months with repeated refusals. Finally, after another "No" vote at a merger meeting, the Call Committee resigned, saying that under the circumstances theirs was a hopeless task. This caused many to change their vote, and the merger was approved with tacit understanding that it would mean a new church.

A better image of the congregation in the minds of its members. The attitude was always one of "getting by" and "it's good enough." It influenced the entire program of the congregation.

It must be noted that the inefficiency and pressure were "surface" reasons and recognized by those who finally approved the merger. The other — and deeper — reasons were recognized by only a few at the start. But as these came into prominence, they became the reasons for building the new church.

Obstacles

There were many obstacles to the merger and to the building.

The history of the congregation. It has had a long and honorable past. In 1850 two Norwegian Lutheran congregations were organized by Pastor H. A. Stub in two rural settlements called Gjerpen and Valders. The first Letter of Call was signed by 124 men. In 1853 there were 50 baptisms a year, and by 1860 there were 100 baptisms a year. This says something about the growth of these early churches as well as the size of the families. Right from the start these have been strong churches, and they have gloried in their past. The two open country churches worshiped in buildings, one of which was built in 1869 and the other in 1874. Several generations have been baptized, confirmed, married, and buried from these buildings. The loyalty here is deep and very understandable. There was apparent reason to praise God for these churches. But the problem lay with identifying the church with the building — and not only the church, but God!

Old animosities. In addition to the deep loyalties to their own congregation, there had been a history of animosity, particularly in one of the congregations where, in the 1890's, a group withdrew and formed a new congregation, to be served by another pastor. It is interesting to note that this was done in 1899, only about two years after a railroad station was established one mile to the east which later became known as the Village of Valders. Perhaps part of this withdrawal was incipient community pride. It was also partly a continuation of an old disagreement. The first resident pastor, J. A. Otteson, wrote in 1853 about the situation in that same church, "There has been a sorry controversy in the matter of selecting a place for the church." To decide the issue, Ole Gigstad and Thomas Thompson Helle were asked to choose a tree of equal girth and the first one to fell his tree could choose the church location. It's interesting to note that it's along these same lines that the split in the congregation took place in 1899. Although it's 65 years later, this is still a deep, rankling issue with some.

Conservatism. This is dairy country, and sociologists tell us that dairymen as a class are one of the most conservative — they would have to be to stay in dairying.

Strengths

What are some of the strengths of the congregation?

Dedicated core of leadership. One cannot underestimate the leavening influence of such a group. Fortunately, they included our most respected people and the most active in community affairs. These were used with responsibility and others were challenged and encouraged. The problem here is that the leadership must see its role in terms of the church as the Body of Christ rather than just another civic organization which contributes "good" to the community.

Long, though very gradual, history of coming together. From the start, the two rural congregations were served by one pastor. The village church, which split from the one rural congregation, was served by a pastor in Manitowoc. In 1940, following the death of one pastor and the resignation of the other, the three congregations merged into a three-point parish. This had been discussed for years. Even then there was a concern for being one congregation. The first real step toward parish unity was the organization of a parish choir in 1940 which sang in the three churches on alternate Sundays. This was followed by a joint Luther League.

School consolidation. In the past ten years, Valders has become the center of a school district which serves 95% of our members. This is a great factor in our unity. The Valders High School football and basketball teams created a great deal of loyalty — more so than ever before because now almost all attend high school. The children became acquainted and found their friends from the whole area rather than just the old country school. The contrast between the old one-room school and the consolidated school was great enough for the people to begin to see that the old systems are not always good enough for our day.

A stable community. Our roots go deep. Many of our farms have been in the same family for over 100 years. Ninety percent of our families have been here for 40 years or more. While not a rich congregation because the majority of its members are dairy farmers, nevertheless there is a stability and consistency of income.

While listed last, it is the most important: *A God who is able to use even us!*

Results

Here are a few of the obvious results of the merger and the new building.

Increased attendance at worship services. Even after the merger, before the erection of the new building, with services held on a rotating basis in two of the churches each Sunday, people tended to attend services at "their own church." With a united congregation in one building, our people are attending church with a much greater consistency. It is also much easier for our Board of Deacons to see where the problems are at this point.

A stronger Sunday school. Fewer teachers are needed and a better division of classes is possible. Facilities are immensely improved. Our whole attitude has changed. Part of this change has been reflected in increased planning on the part of our Board of Education as well as other boards. We plan now how to make the best use of our facilities, and there is much discussion about what else we need to be more effective in our teaching. This planning is shown by the fact that on the very first Sunday of Sunday school in the new building there was absolutely no confusion and no lost teaching time. Within a month, additional equipment had been purchased and other changes made to correct situations which before we would have just "lived with."

A sense of pride in our church and congregation. I think this is a healthy attitude. It gives an optimistic outlook for the work of the congregation. We dare to attempt more for Christ now. It is interesting to meet with the various boards and to see now the attitude of positive concern coupled with the feeling that they should try new ways and do their best.

Strengthening of our community. It has done much for our community to have a church that the "city people" come to look at and envy. Rural people are too often apologetic for being rural. Our church has given new stature to our rural area. It has made our community a more attractive place to live.

Greater loyalty of high school age and post high youth. It is most inspiring to see this age group at worship and Sunday school.

Services to the entire congregation. With but few exceptions, our aged and infirm are able to attend church. I have almost no calls on shut-ins.

Warm feet. Those of you who have served in a typical rural church know what I mean when I say it has made a difference to have warm feet all winter long.

Basic Premise

There has been one basic premise overriding this entire pastoral approach. For it I want to pay tribute to Dr. E. W. Mueller, for I have been profoundly influenced by him. He writes, "The congregation will need to define its role more precisely. I have the conviction that the church must do less, but that it must do its precise task more adequately. At the same time the congregation must broaden its concern. Its concern for people must be as broad as God's concern for people. This concern need not always be expressed through church structures. It can be expressed through many other structures. If the church will pursue this approach it will again occupy a position in the community that will enable it to give direction to community leadership." This has become the rationale for our new church — to serve our community as only we can serve it.

Principles

There were certain principles practiced as we attempted to put this program into being.

The pastor must have confidence in the members of the congregation even though by past experience they have indicated no confidence in themselves.

The pastor must earn the right to be the pastor by a faithful ministry in Word and Sacrament. Such a pastor will be loved by his people and always listened to. He may not always be heeded, but he will be heard.

The pastor must understand and love his people. Here, hard work the first days in the parish gave me a several years' head start. For the first ten days I did nothing but call in the 350 homes of the congregation. Members of the church council of the three congregations lined up 20-minute home calls for me beginning at 8 in the morning and continuing until 11 at night. In every home I had devotions, met the family, and got acquainted.

Confidence in the rural community needs to be encouraged.

Despite all the gloom and despair about our rural areas, I have complete confidence in ours.

The pastor must have a clear-cut goal. The pastor needs to study the situation and to have a clear idea of what he hopes to accomplish.

Go slow. Sometimes people are asked to make too big a decision too soon. They should not decide more than needs to be decided at each stage. It is better to make a series of decisions which start small and increase in importance. Thus, we avoided lengthy tirades which put a man in a public position from which he could hardly back down. We never had a congregational meeting to vote on an issue until we were sure how the vote would go.

A worthy challenge is needed. For us, the challenge was the new church. Perhaps the reason some congregations are so interested in bazaars and suppers is that they have nothing else to do. It's not a money problem. It's a problem of commitment. Just to give money for a budget is not very thrilling unless the program represented by that budget is exciting. Our congregation doubled its giving in one year when the decision to build was made.

Strive for excellence. We set our sights high in our building program. We wanted a church that would be a witness to Christ in our community. A year was spent searching for an architect. The Building Committee worked hard. The pastor insisted on the use of good art, and the sculptor who was commissioned has made an outstanding contribution to the artistic quality of the building.

Respect for the past is important. This is best indicated by the fact that the final services held in the three old buildings were included in the bulletin with the dedication of the new church. The old churches were "closed to the glory of God," even as we dedicated the new church to the glory of God.

Deal in love with all. There must be no hint of personal disapproval by the pastor of any individual who disagrees with him or who opposes the program. They must all be loved in Christ by their pastor.

The Continuing Mission

At the beginning of this presentation I said that the congregation faces two critical issues — to be relevant and to have something to say.

Faith Lutheran Church is speaking more relevantly to its day and locale than before. Therefore, what we have to say is more important than ever before because now more people are ready to listen.

Grateful and proud of what we have already accomplished by God's grace, we are thus challenged to stretch even farther as the people of God in Valders — with God's Word for our day.

18.

Howard A. Lenhardt

The Suburban Challenge

Paul, in his Second Letter to the Corinthians, states: "Such is the confidence that we have through Christ toward God. Not that we are sufficient of ourselves to claim anything as coming from us, our sufficiency is from God, who has qualified us to be ministers of a new covenant, not in a written code, but in the Spirit" — and thus he alludes to the primary mission of the church.

Good Shepherd, Buena Park, California, is, we pray, a congregation in mission; a congregation that is highly aware of its mission through assignment by Christ himself to build his kingdom. To preach and teach and live according to the Gospel of Christ, with lives consecrated to his call and service is the ultimate and basic goal of the people of God. Here men are called to faith and repentance. From here the people of God go forth to live, after personal confrontation with the Christ through Word and Sacrament, lives wholly dedicated to his service, to be truly the people of God, the ministers of the new covenant who find their sufficiency in God himself.

This description of the congregation in mission is perhaps more hope than fact, more ideal than actual, but nevertheless, it is, in ultimate, this congregation truly endeavoring to function as the Body of Christ, the people of God, the Communion of Saints.

Good Shepherd, Buena Park, California, as a congregation is comparatively new. Organized in 1956 with a little less than 100 adult confirmed members, it has grown in these 9½ years to a congregation of over 1,000 confirmed members and over 1,800 baptized members. We might say that in the past three years it has gone through a period not unlike the gangling growth period of early adolescence, having just about doubled its size. It has moved from 500 confirmed members in 1962 to slightly over 1,000 during 1965. During this three-year period, 692 adults have been received into membership, 196 adult losses were recorded, for a net growth of 496 confirmed members. Baptized membership has grown by a net of 800 persons. Adults have been received as follows: baptism 57; confirmation 254; transfer 311; reaffirmation 70. Average attendance at worship has grown also, from 300 per Sunday to just under 600 per Sunday.

The immediate community of Buena Park has grown from 1,500 persons in 1950 to 54,000 persons in 1960 to an estimated 65,000 persons in 1965. Its area of responsibility probably embraces in excess of 100,000 persons. The end of population growth is unpredictable at this writing; however, it is expected that the population of Orange County will double to in excess of 2 million persons by 1975.

Because of the tremendous growth prospective and because of the inability of a one-man full-time staff to cope with this growth potential, the Board of American Missions assisted in the placement of a parish worker in February of 1963 while the congregation was still under salary aid assistance. This addition to the staff opened even more potential, and in October of 1963 the parish worker was replaced with a team-ministry program with the addition of another pastor to the staff. The Board of American Missions assumed the full cost of this addition to the program for the first nine months, two-thirds of the cost for the next six months, one-half of the cost for the next twelve months, after which it is expected that the congregation will assume the full cost of the team-ministry program.

The Pastor's Role

In the team-ministry program, the assistant pastor is responsible for the Christian education program, the evangelism program, and the youth program, and meets with the corresponding committees of the congregation in the planning of these programs. The senior pastor is responsible for the overall program of the congregation, meets with all other committees and plans the preaching program; however, the assistant pastor preaches at about 40 percent of the services. Both pastors are present at all services; however, the liturgist for a particular Sunday often leaves the service at the sermon hymn to observe in the Sunday church school. Three services and three sessions of the Sunday church school are conducted each Sunday, meeting at 8:00 A.M., 9:30 A.M. and 11:00 A.M.

The job analysis of the pastors of Good Shepherd, approved by the church council and the congregation is, as follows:

The pastors' primary responsibility is the care of souls. In doing this, they shall:

1. Proclaim the Word through preaching, teaching and personal Christian witness

2. Administer the Sacraments and thus:
   a. Nurture the people of God in the Christian Faith;
   b. Relate that faith in Christ to everyday life;
   c. Comfort and counsel in time of spiritual need.

3. Develop the program of the congregation
   a. Guide the church staff.
      1. Administration
      2. Leadership training
   b. Guide and develop the educational program of the congregation.
   c. Supervise the administration of the physical plant.
   d. Administer the overall program of the congregation.

4. Integrate the congregation into a working unit of God's kingdom so that members become aware that they are the people of God, God's colony in man's world.

The preaching program at Good Shepherd generally revolves around the pericopes for each particular Sunday of the church year. This insures that the pastors touch on all the pertinent doctrines of the church as they are related through the Scriptures. However, this does not exclude from the pulpit items of particular current concern. The pulpit cannot and does not ignore the world of the community and its inherent problems. If the people of God are to be effective witnesses in their lives, they must be trained to let the influence of God's Word be pertinent in their everyday lives. Often the pastors draw upon current national and community events to illustrate the need of bringing Christ out of the church building into the market place.

Recently a pastor's sermon seminar, consisting of 10 to 15 invited persons has conducted a "brainstorming" session on the appointed lessons for a Sunday one week in advance. The group meets on Wednesday evenings with the pastor assigned to preach 10 days later.

It is hoped that through this seminar-type approach, the pastors can become more aware of the everyday problems facing the average parishioner. With the help of the Holy Spirit, without whose guidance and direction nothing can really be done in the church, it is hoped that this seminar group can help the pulpit interpret questions people are asking, rather than speaking, often vaguely, to questions people aren't really concerned about.

Much pastoral time is spent in personal consultation concerning problems in human relations, from marital difficulties to personal problems, from youth concerns to old-age security, from mental anxiety to spiritual bankruptcy. When necessary, referrals are made and psychological and psychiatric help is obtained. A Christian psychologist has been added recently to the staff on a part-time basis. This program is now only beginning, so we cannot evaluate it at this time. A local unit of Recovery Inc. will begin using church facilities in the near future. An Alcoholic Anonymous group is also using church facilities for two weekly meetings. In addition to pastoral counseling by appointment and otherwise, each pastor endeavors to make a minimum of 75 pastoral calls per month in the homes or in the hospital in cases where parishioners are physically ill.

In the community the pastors are active in the Ministerial Association, the Lutheran Hospital Board, the United Fund

Committee and on a rotation system with other pastors of the community to open the City Council meetings with prayer.

Committee Structure

Stewardship of time, talents, and means is emphasized throughout the year in sermons, writings, tracts, and announcements. The stewardship committee meets bimonthly and endeavors to oversee the stewardship emphasis of the congregation. At the every member visitation, cottage meetings, or stewardship dinners, members of the congregation are urged to complete a check-list of talents and interests. These are tabulated and the various committee heads are given the names of individuals interested in serving on their particular committee. Approximately 250 persons are engaged in active participation in the various committees, choirs, and teaching staff. Involvement on the part of even more people is desired and it is hoped that an expanding program can accomplish this fact.

Over the past three years, congregational giving has increased from $37,000 in 1962 to $50,000 in 1963 to $80,000 in 1964. Income for 1965 should be in excess of $84,000. Benevolence giving has moved from 50% of the apportionment in 1962 to 96% in 1964 and will probably reach 100% in 1965.

The worship committee functions in the assignments of ushers and acolytes. The congregation's three choir directors, three organists, acolyte mother, Lutheran Church Women and altar chairwoman, together with other appointees, serve on this committee. Once during the year a commentary narrative service is conducted to keep the congregation aware of the meaning of the liturgy, and occasionally during the year questions concerning the liturgy are answered during congregational announcements or in the newsletter which is mailed monthly to the homes of members and prospective members and Sunday church school parents.

In its social ministry program the congregation has established its own blood bank, has a harvest ingathering appeal for the Home for the Aged, and endeavors to be aware of the physical needs of members suffering from misfortune. The pastors have a small discretionary fund which can be used in time of emergency. The semi-annual Lutheran World Action Appeal also comes under the direction of this committee.

The Christian education committee meets regularly and participates actively in the planning and carrying out of this important phase of the congregation's mission. It endeavors to encourage religious education for adults as well as children. Plans are made and carried out not only for Sunday church school, but also for total Christian family education. Over 600 are enrolled in the Sunday church school and the new curriculum of the Lutheran Church in America is being utilized as soon as the various courses are released for congregational use. A staff of over 60 administers and teaches in church school. Three sessions are held each Sunday with Junior High School and High School Youth meeting at 8:00 A.M. and with duplicate sessions for Beginners through 6th Grades held at 9:30 and 11:00 A.M. To further augment youth education, a weekday church school for 3rd, 4th, 5th, and 6th graders has been initiated. The Family Education Series of the LCA is followed in the weekday school. Teacher training is required of all who serve in any educational function in the congregation.

Confirmation classes meet 1½ hours on Saturday mornings. Youth confirmation is preceded by three years of instruction, beginning at the 7th grade and culminating at the 9th grade.

We realize that we still have a long way to go in adult formal education and the committee continues to wrestle with this problem. One means of adult education is *The Lutheran* which is mailed to every home.

A youth council oversees the youth program of the congregation. This program consists of a Junior High Luther League, a Senior High Luther League and a College and Career Unmarried Young Adult Group. These groups meet the first three Sunday evenings of each month, with the exception of the latter which meets monthly. Traditional programs are followed and approximately 75 to 100 youth participate.

The evangelism thrust is directed by an active committee.

This outreach of the congregation begins often through personal invitation on a person-to-person basis, bringing someone else to worship or to Sunday church school. Enrollment in Sunday church school or attendance at worship begins the process of formal contact. A personal letter is sent by the pastors upon the first visit at worship. A second visit initiates a pastoral call. Discussion ascertains the interest of an individual or family concerning their becoming a part of this congregation. Those of non-Lutheran background are required to attend a series of six pastor's classes, usually held on Sunday evenings. All new members are requested to attend an orientation meeting. They are invited to the meeting by a shepherd family. This family accompanies the new members to the orientation meeting and also on the Sunday when they are received into membership. Coffee is served on the church patio when new members are received, and members are urged to make acquaintance and welcome these new persons in the faith. Some identification, usually a flower, is pinned on the new members, so they can be readily welcomed. Once every three months, a Friendly Visitor Sunday gathers together some 60 to 70 persons who, aftei lunch at church, go to the homes of prospective members inviting them to become a part of this fellowship in Christ.

An active Lutheran Church Women's Auxiliary, a Couples Club of Good Shepherd and a bowling league round out the organizational program of the congregation. The latter two, while being basically social, fulfill a very necessary function in the life of the parish as the people of God are brought together and often form lasting and enduring friendships.

A church council of fifteen men and women, together with both pastors, directs and oversees the active program of the congregation. To them falls the responsibility to keep this parish constantly pointed in the direction of the Christ.

The program is carried on in a first unit built and occupied since 1960, primarily to serve in the ultimate as an educational building. It consists of pastors' studies, church office, five classrooms, and an all-purpose room which can accommodate 250 to 300 at worship. Plans are being developed to erect the permanent church building during 1968.

Good Shepherd parish engages itself in a lot of activity which we pray is not mere human activity, but is actively directed by the Holy Spirit of God working in and through the lives of a dedicated and consecrated people. Its main emphasis is that God was in Christ reconciling the world to himself. Its strength comes only through the recognition of Christ as Lord and Savior. To him be the glory and the power. From him come the people of God and through him the people of God express themselves in this parish and from this parish go forth into the world.

19.

Form
Follows
Function

A. Karl Boehmke

"Form follows function" — if anywhere, certainly in the church. How dare there be wasted time or manpower if the mission of Christ is to be accomplished? Let church organization be as contemporary as the new architecture. God has allowed us to know the secret of his plan: He proposes that all human history shall be consummated in Christ, that everything shall find its fulfillment in him (Eph. 1:9, 10).

The parish is still a hand of Christ in history. Some will assert that the parish has outlived its day. Perhaps so. If something better is to be had, we should not hesitate to build it. Meanwhile the earthen vessel had best be shaped to maximum effectiveness for Christ's work on the contemporary scene.

Functions Five

Let us start with the functions (what the life of the parish centers around) reduced to the minimum:

1. Growth in worship
2. Growth in education
3. Growth in evangelism
4. Growth in stewardship
5. Growth in works of mercy

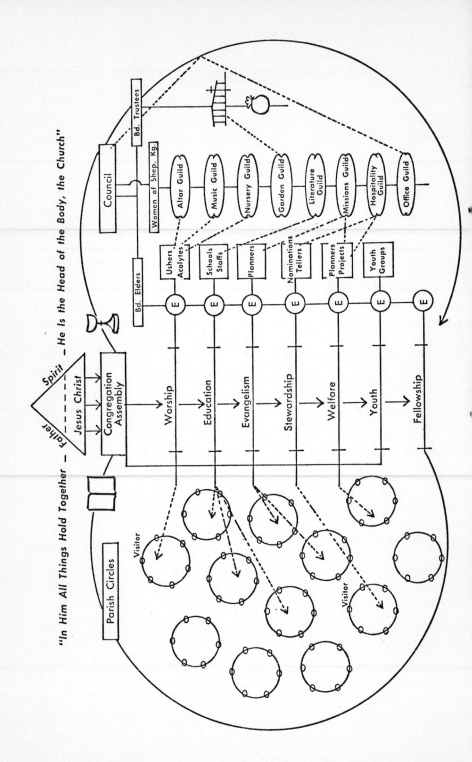

"In Him All Things Hold Together" — He Is the Head of the Body, the Church"

Father — Jesus Christ — Spirit

Congregation Assembly

Worship
Education
Evangelism
Stewardship
Welfare
Youth
Fellowship

Parish Circles

Visitor

Council
Bd. Trustees
Bd. Elders
Women of Shep. Kg.

Altar Guild
Music Guild
Nursery Guild
Garden Guild
Literature Guild
Missions Guild
Hospitality Guild
Office Guild

Ushers Acolytes
Schools Staffs
Planners
Nominations Tellers
Planners Projects
Youth Groups

The body of Christ achieves its objectives through attention to all five. Growth in fellowship may also be counted but stands in a different, supportive relationship to the others.

Christ the Head

The congregation receives its commission, its authority, from Jesus Christ. He is the Head, the Commander. Some of his orders are general, ongoing. But the specific orders of the day must be seen in the light of current history and current society. The body must be growing and training for tomorrow at the same time that it is reaching out for his objectives today.

Key Planning Posts

At the Church of the Shepherd King in Birmingham, Michigan, each elder is charged with one specific key function. All activities of the congregation and subordinate groups touching on this function are his responsibility.

The elder for worship is concerned with the worship services of the congregation at large but also with the worship of various committees and guilds, worship of the families in their homes, joint worship with other Christian groups. He is responsible for the director of music, the choirs, ushers, acolytes, altar attendants.

The elder for education is responsible for all educational activities, whether in the pastor's classes, parish Bible groups, youth Bible classes, children's schools, or joint educational activities with other congregations or schools.

The elder for evangelism is concerned with the entire mission outreach of the church through its parish circles, youth, or children's groups. He links the congregation to the broad world mission of Christ through public relations and the many mission arms of the metropolitan council, district, synod, and church at large. He looks to the winning of one soul and the winning of the world.

The elder for stewardship is responsible for helping the members to develop their baptismal talents in the service of

Christ. He is chairman of the nominations committee, which functions throughout the year, selecting people for offices and offices for people who need to keep on growing in grace. Since daily labor is seen as key service for Christ, he helps families relate their life plans and projects to the objectives of Christ through their weekly monetary gifts to the church and works of mercy. He keeps the budget at the foot of the cross.

The elder for Christian welfare lays the concerns of Christ upon the hearts of his people for the healing of the sick, feeding of the hungry, housing of the homeless, visiting of the prisoners. He interprets the organizations and institutions of the larger church to the local congregation. He studies the causes of human welfare in the community, again interpreting them in the light of the Christian calling and the support of the church people.

The elder for parish fellowship recognizes that families need to be grouped together so that the aims of Christ may be understood and the power of the Holy Spirit put into concrete motion. He is the right-hand man to the other elders, providing a structure for the operational phases of their work.

Youth of the church in America are a part of the congregation also. Moreover, they are able to encompass all the functions of the church at their particular level. The elder for youth is their spiritual guide, responsible for their development in all areas. He helps them maintain their own stewardship records, develop their Bible study program and service projects with a generous emphasis on fellowship activities.

All basic activities of the congregation are thus under the continuous care and supervision of these seven elders. These men form their own committees, teams, guilds, or leagues to help project the work of the church. The subordinate units are flexible in nature, expanding or contracting according to need.

Properties and Money

Three trustees are charged with the supervision and development of church properties and monetary funds.

Elders and trustees alike are elected by the congregational

assembly. Here both men and women vote to delegate authority
into the hands of the council members. Twice each year the assembly meets for elections, to review the work of the whole
church, and to adopt plans for future activities. Meanwhile the
council remains in monthly session.

Women's Activities

The women of the church serve in significant ways according to their specialized abilities. They work under the supervision
of the specific elders or trustees concerned with their services.

The altar guild, music guild, and nursery guild relate to the
elder for worship. Missions guild and hospitality guild relate
both to the elder for evangelism and the elder for Christian welfare. Literature guild comes under the elder for education. Garden guild is the green thumb of the properties trustee, while the
office guild serves the general secretary of the congregation.
Guilds may form or dissolve from time to time according to need.

Each guild has a chairman chosen by its own members, also
a secretary-treasurer. These chairmen and a handful of presiding
officers form the women's board to coordinate all women's activities and arrange for a few combined activities in the course of
the year.

Parish Circles

Two keys to the parish circle structure are fellowship and
flexibility. Neighbors are grouped together, five to eight families
in a circle. (Occasionally some will go larger.) As the church
membership changes, circle patterns change — a new circle forms,
an older one is absorbed, a growing circle splits.

Since circles remain small, no circle visitor needs to oversee
more than a handful of families. Appointed by the elder for fellowship and the council, these visitors develop a pastoral concern
for their families. They hope to see their members grow in the
functions that relate them to the body of Christ.

In certain general functions the value of the circles is evident. When the news of illness or death needs to be circulated,

here is the channel. When any family suffers illness or bereavement or has some special joy, there is a specific group of Christian neighbors who feel their close responsibility to express sympathy in tangible ways.

But the circle objective goes far beyond this. It offers a practical framework for carrying out the projects of the church. When the elder for evangelism needs to relate a new family to the church, he knows exactly whom to call. When he plans a major evangelism thrust, all circles may be called in. The elder for education carries lay Bible study into the homes through the circles. Circle representatives meet with the pastor for briefing on Sunday, then gather the circles in the homes during the week. At year's end the circles gather to hear the elder for stewardship talk of God's inexpressible Gift. The elder for welfare sets up clothing depots in circle homes for distribution through metropolitan agencies or world relief.

The Key

The entire parish structure is aimed at specific Christian goals. Organization is minimal and flexible. Responsibility is pinpointed. Originality and imagination are encouraged. Here the pastor is no administrator but rather a counselor. His chief concern is that Christians may be properly equipped for their service, that the whole body may be built up (Eph. 4:12). The goal is to grow up in every way into Christ, the Head. For it is from the Head that the whole body, as a harmonious structure knit together by the joints with which it is provided, grows by the proper functioning of individual parts to its full maturity in love (Eph. 4:15, 16).

20.

Robert E. Neumeyer

The Whole Church in the Whole Community

How can we be the whole church in the whole community? What I have to say will be based largely on a report of what has happened in Philadelphia in the past thirteen months. It will center heavily on the inner city, but with the full realization that it has implications for those who are not in the inner city.

The Diverse Community

First of all, I would like to sketch for you the community of Center City Lutheran Parish in Philadelphia. From the standpoint of geography we cover the heart of inner Philadelphia. In this heart are 28 Lutheran congregations — 27 LCA, and 1 Missouri Synod. A generation ago there were 40 Lutheran congregations in this same area. Interestingly enough, Lutheran churches have all but disappeared in the large, so-called riot section of this great city. Only one Lutheran church remains to witness in this section. From a racial standpoint it has been estimated that nearly 800,000 Negroes live in metropolitan Philadelphia today. The vast majority of them are jammed into this area we call Center City Parish. With them are also about 35,000 Puerto Ricans. If we were to take an overlay of the so-called poverty area of the city of Philadelphia, we would find that these twelve pockets of poverty would be almost identical with the so-called geographical outline of Center City Parish. This means that the average family income of all the people in this territory we call Center City Parish is under $3,000 a year family income, and the median education level is somewhere between the 7th and 8th grade.

Twenty of the twenty-seven Lutheran churches in this community are racially integrated. Almost every one of our church buildings is a hand-me-down that is left over from another generation, and is almost unbelievably expensive to maintain. One, for example, took $35,000 from its dwindling endowment fund to hold up a steeple of a building that seats 1,200. I recently preached there two Sundays ago to 51 people. I could take you to another place where they spent $5,000 to repair a heating system. They average 92 people per Sunday in church. Now what has happened is that in almost every instance these large buildings are empty because the white people have left them to the Negro. Ten of our congregations are receiving subsidy from the national body.

In our parish area there are some of the worst slums in Philadelphia. We have high-rise, low-rent apartments in some other sections. In the general community which is Center City Parish, there are pockets of the pitiful. There are alcoholics, dope addicts, and a great concentration of homosexuals. There are even special clubs for this latter group.

In this same geographical area there are also three large centers of education — the University of Pennsylvania, Temple University, and Drexel Institute of Technology. There are 3,500 art and music students, hospitals with nursing schools and medical schools, high-rise apartments with the doormen and everything else you associate with the affluent, wealthy society.

We have in this geographical area the centers of political power. We also have all of the headquarters of the prominent civil rights groups — both the radical and the conservative. In this same geographical area we have certain white strongholds — little white islands that are holding out against the racial movement and shift in the city. Now, when I speak of a whole community, it is a community that is not an isolated little neighborhood, but many neighborhoods with many kinds of people. The man who lives in the ghetto may sweep the streets in the high-rise area, but the high-rise area is still a part of his total community. People work outside of the little communities in the bigger community, and what they see on the outside they reflect upon. The people who live in the other areas also reflect upon the ghettos. I am afraid that sometimes in our zeal for an inner-city ministry, and in our emphasis upon the community, we forget that there is always a relationship between the ghetto and the high-rise and the suburbs which cannot be ignored. Until we see the whole community this way, I don't think we see a community at all.

Within this community, however, three attitudes seem to be rather impressive in the way they stand out. There is a feeling of increasing hostility to the church. There is an appalling ignorance, as we observe it, of the church and Christianity, and a certain indifference which is frightening.

One young pastor who was working in the riot section of north Philadelphia saw some very young teen-age girls about 13 or 14 years old. Since he was running a teen-canteen at his church, he casually walked over to the girls and said, "Would you like to come over to the canteen tonight?" The one girl, barely 14, looked him straight in the eye and said, "Why don't you take your God damned Jesus Christ and go to hell — we don't want him."

In a backyard of one of our inner-city areas there is a little tree. It has been struggling to survive — but it's there. Swinging on the lowest branch of this tree was a little boy about five years old. The woman who owned the little house came out and said, "Sonny, please don't swing on the branch of the tree. You might break it and you wouldn't want to hurt the tree because it belongs to God." The little fellow looked at her without batting an eye, and without attempting to be smart said very simply, "Who is God?" These may be unusual examples, but I am convinced that they speak of the two great problems that we have in this whole community — hostility toward the church and what it has stood for over the past years, and ignorance of Christ and the message of the church. Naturally this makes for indifference in other areas too. I happen to believe that this kind of hostility and ignorance exists in the suburbs too, just as it exists in the high-rise apartments in Center City, Philadelphia. Many times, however, this is covered up by a fine veneer which hides the ugly reality.

The Wholeness of the Church

Now, in this whole community, how can we possibly be the whole church? There are several observations which I think need to be made before we can adequately answer this question. One is that the church as an institution is here now, and we had better prepare to live with it for a while and to renew what we have. No matter how hard some people try to imagine it away, it is going to be here for a long time as an institution. Therefore, in our work as the whole church in the whole community, we dare not forget this and bypass existing structures for new forms which are not going to be here next year or the year after.

Secondly, the church in terms of special ministries is also here. I personally believe that all of the so-called special ministries are somehow related to the whole church. I can see the crying need for special ministries to addicts and homosexuals and gangs, but somehow I feel there must be a relationship to the organized church structure.

The church in the suburbs is here, and I am a little bit tired of people simply kicking it around, because I believe there is a restlessness in suburbia whereby it senses that it belongs to the whole community which is the city. It is not quite sure which way it should go or speak or help, but somehow it yearns to be part of the Body of Christ. What I am saying is that whether the church is "an institutional type," or a special ministry approach, or whether it is in confused suburbia, we had better learn that we are all members of the same Body, and that the arm cannot do without the leg. There is a temptation to church workers in the inner city and to pastors in suburbia to forget this very simple biblical statement that "together we are the Body of Christ." There is a lack of understanding on both sides, and I think we must do everything possible to build an understanding of how we need each other because we belong together in Christ.

Cooperative Ministry

Now somehow we must learn to be the whole church to the whole community. So we have in Philadelphia an experiment which is unique perhaps because of its size and some of its programming. We have a large cooperative ministry, which is basically a federation of congregations. These twenty-seven congregations in the geographical community I described were invited to join Center City Parish. Twenty-three of the twenty-seven voted to join. Now all of these twenty-three congregations operate on their own, with their own treasuries, budgets, pastors, and programs. Liturgically they range from high church extremes to the lowest church expression. Their ministry ranges all the way from gang work among Negroes to work with middle-class and upper-middle class Negroes. They operate their own program, but they cooperate on other things. They work together on things that they feel they can do better together. One small illustration is a matter of buying oil. By having a bulk oil purchase plan we have saved about $3,000 to $4,000 in one year. Obviously this is something they can do better together. We are different from some of the other cooperative ministries which are being set up in various cities because we cover a large geographical area, and because we are so many congregations. Frankly, this is an effort to find another kind of answer, because sooner or later we have got to be realistic about what this kind of thing costs. I think all of us are apprehensive about what these other kinds of ministries are going to cost and who is going to pay the bill.

We must learn to be the whole church in the whole community, to work cooperatively, and yet be sensible in terms of what this will mean in other cities — not only cities of two million, but cities of three or four hundred thousand.

Downtown Center

Center City Lutheran Parish is the sponsoring agency for a Lutheran information and counseling center in downtown Philadelphia. This information and counseling center is on one of the busiest streets in Philadelphia. It is next to one of the largest motion picture theaters in the city, which has an attendance of a quarter to a half-million people a year. Millions of people pass by our door during the course of a year, and they see a display in the window of artwork, carvings, and books. They see a sign which says there are books for buying or for browsing. Indeed, we do have books to sell. This is a gimmick because this area is a little book happy. Everybody wants to read the latest little paperbacks. There is a sign which says that this is a Lutheran information and counseling center, and that we are open from 9:00 A.M. until 9:00 P.M., Monday through Saturday.

Sometimes people wander in and pretend to look at books with one eye, but they are looking at me with the other eye as if to say, "Is this the kind of guy I'd like to talk to?" In one year 5,000 people have come in to this information center. It is fortunate that they didn't all have problems, but we have had 400 counseling sessions. Last week a Buddhist from South Vietnam came in to talk about the meaning of Christianity, since he was finding Buddhism to be rather shallow. We have had Mohammedans and Jews and atheists and Roman Catholics. We have had all kinds of problems — the kind that you meet in the parish ministry from the suicidal depressives to marital problems, but many are different in that we get only one opportunity to counsel with them. We allow them to remain completely anonymous. This counseling situation often attracts the lesbian and the homosexual. We have people who belong to Lutheran congregations in Center City Parish. We have Lutherans from the suburbs The other day I had a pastor's wife come in to talk to me about her marriage problems. So we have had a great variety of situations for counseling.

Now this is rather important in terms of the image to these twenty-three congregations. In a very real way, since this is also the main office for Center City Parish, this relates them immediately to the whole community. It is not just their small area in the heart of one of Philadelphia's many slums, but it is their slum congregation that is also related to this counseling and information center which gives them a sense of pride and a little different image. Center City Parish works directly with pastors and church councils. We give counsel and guidance to individuals as they face need in their particular congregations.

We have now for the first time in Philadelphia a Negro pastor serving what is presently an all-white congregation. This is the first time that there has been a Negro serving any denomination's white congregation in the city of Philadelphia. This congregation, a small one, is in the heart of a Negro-Puerto Rican area. I counseled with them and showed them how they fit into the strategy of the Center City Parish. I pointed out to them that if they did not witness to this community, there would be no Lutheran witness at all in a large geographic area. When I asked about their outreach they said, "Oh, we're willing to have them, but they just don't come." Then I suggested that their image may be bad and that they could change this by having a Negro pastor. When we picked the pieces off the ceiling, they finally began to see that they were part of a whole and that they were related to other congregations in the larger community. The result was that they voted unanimously as a congregation to ask the Board to assign the Negro pastor to their congregation. Now I am convinced that without someone to show them their place in the framework of the whole church in the whole community, this could never have happened.

We have another congregation located in a community which has been entirely rebuilt, and which has a history dating back to Pre-Revolutionary days. We won't even have the prostitutes and the drunks to minister to anymore. So this congregation is beginning to examine its mission. In talking with a typical board member, who is 85 years old, about the future of the congregation, I showed him the map, the work, and the witness we were trying to carry out as a whole. He suddenly looked up and said, "Vell, if ve stay as ve are, ve'll be a dead church —

if ve try your vay ve might be the living church." He was 85 years old, German through and through, but he was beginning to see that he was a part of the whole church. I think this could not happen outside of the perspective of Center City Parish.

Social Concerns

We seek to spur involvement on various levels. In the field of race relations we encourage congregations to witness as they are able. This may mean participating in the various civil rights groups so that they can have a voice instead of always standing on the sidelines and complaining, or it may mean assisting in breaking down barriers. We are very much concerned that several of our congregations which are now all-white are going to be faced within six months or six years with a Negro movement that is going to set their neighborhoods on fire. We are trying to prepare these congregations now for this change which will surely come. It is amazing to see how they are beginning to understand the Negro, and we had better learn to understand them, because it is estimated that nearly a half million of metropolitan Philadelphia's Negroes are unchurched. The truth is that we have managed somehow to pull out of the areas in the city where the Negro population is most massive.

In two areas we had the cooperation of pastors and congregations, and we said, "Now is the time to make a move." Never before had they moved outside of their own immediate membership. They had never made an evangelism call around the block because around the block were Negroes and Puerto Ricans. Within one year we have broken down barriers in two such congregations, and it looks as though they are going to live and live wonderfully well in their witness.

We encourage involvement in such things as the Poverty Program. The city of Philadelphia had a rather interesting plan whereby the poverty area was divided into twelve sections. Each of these sections had a meeting. Eleven of these meetings were held in public schools. One of them was held in a Lutheran church. This didn't happen by accident. It happened because I was interested in the poverty program, and in getting to know some of its officials in downtown Philadelphia. It was a real thrill to see this old German church, which used to average about 18 or 19 people at worship on Sunday, jammed with 600 to 800 people. It was especially interesting when a couple of women from the Ladies Aid came in to see what was going on and they saw the entertainment which preceded the business. The entertainment was five boys in leopard skin costumes beating bongo drums. This was quite an innovation for a church that still has a German service. I think one of the thrills of my life was when I broke through the bureaucracy on the night of these poverty meetings. This was the initial thrust on the part of the mayor's committee to get into the communities and explain the program. I finally got the pastors of the district to demand that the district meeting, which was scheduled for the same night, be postponed. This was something new — to think that the poor of the community were more important than the bureaucratic machinery of the church. The district meeting was held about a week or two later.

Seven of our churches are participating in the Get-Set Program. This is the preschool and child-day-care program. These services are being offered in congregations that used to have their church doors open only on Sunday for two hours. Now they are open Monday through Friday from 7:00 A.M. to 5:30 P.M. We had made a proposal of our own to operate child day-care centers and preschool education programs. It was turned down because it was not large enough. Instead of running away and saying, "They don't want to play our game so we won't play with them," we turned right around and I was invited, since I had made the proposal for Center City Parish, to participate in future discussions. They asked whether our churches might lend their facilities for this program. So I served as the spokesman and the intermediary there so that our congregations might be involved.

We have other programs which spur involvement. We have a little news sheet which is strictly an effort to build a unity of purpose and to share and promote ideas related to race, poverty, and community programs.

Seminary Involvement

The Lutheran seminary in Philadelphia cooperates with the Center City Lutheran Parish in several ways. In our first year four interns were assigned to the parish. This year we have seven. This new intern program is an experiment as an alternative to a fourth full year of internship. This permits the seminarians to do their senior work in the third year and work five days a week in the parish and two full days and nights at the seminary. These interns are assigned to Center City Parish, and then immediately reassigned by the director to congregations. They work under the immediate supervision of the pastor of the congregation. I receive the weekly reports which indicate the amount of time spent on evangelism, sick calling, and community organizations. We meet as a group once a month, and usually the men come in to see me at least one other time during that same month. This has helped in two ways. It has helped to give us some staff which we desperately need in these situations, and it has also helped to give, at least in Philadelphia Seminary, meaningful training to men who are interested in working in the inner city.

We are also cooperative in certain kinds of field assignments. Nine seminarians have made nearly 3,000 calls in seven different sections of Center City Parish. Within two days the racial barrier was broken in one congregation, and within two weeks it was broken in another. In this house-to-house visitation these men learned some things about the inner city that they could never have garnered from books.

Summer Volunteers

Center City Lutheran Parish also mounts direct programs, the largest of which is a summer Bible day camp. Bible study, centered around the church building itself, was held three mornings a week. On two days the children were taken on trips which provided recreation and education. We served nearly 500 children — 200 of whom had never before been inside a Lutheran church. In order to staff the camp, 33 college and seminary students were brought in. They were paid a total of $200, and

provided with room, board, and transportation. Each student was
asked to visit weekly in the home of his pupil. Now it is pretty
obvious that most of these college young people who served as
counselors came from upper-middle class families or they could
not have afforded to come to work with us. These young people
served magnificently. Each one had a group of seven children for
three weeks, and he indeed became the big brother or the big
sister or the mother or the father figure for many of these children. They went as a group to church or Sunday school at least
once during that three-week period. The carry-over has been
amazing. In two areas we now have active Sunday schools where
a year ago, in one case, there was none; and in another case there
was an enrollment of only 25. The pastors say that this direct
programming, in this particular instance, helped their outreach.

In direct programming we attempt to stimulate both inreach
and outreach, but not to take the place of the ministry of the
pastor or the congregation. When the Youth Commission offered
to make the services of fifteen youth missioners available to the
Center City Parish for orientation in Philadelphia, we assigned
them to recruiting for the summer camp. We initiated a program
of "street corner Bible story telling" in some of the worst slums
of Philadelphia. The missioners would sit on the steps of a house,
on the front steps of the church, or on a street corner, and tell
a Bible story to as many children as they could gather around
them. One young man from California decided to tell the story
of Daniel and the lions' den with chalk. He sat on the curb and
drew a picture of a lion on the asphalt street. The children who
were there thought it was a pretty stupid-looking lion. So he
said, "All right, you draw one." Before long there were lions all
up and down the street, but there were also children who were
listening when he said, "By the way, kids, you know there is more
stuff like this in the church down the street beginning on Monday." And it worked.

Suburban Volunteers

A new experience of the Center City Parish is a Saturday day
camp, staffed by persons from the parish and the suburbs. Its

curriculum includes religious instruction, arts, and crafts, and it will also feature educational trips. For years suburbanites have been delighted to come in to the city and put on a Christmas party or wrap up soap and dolls. So when I preach in suburbia and I am asked, "What can we do," I say, "Be involved in depth for four Saturdays in a row." When you work from 9:30 in the morning till 4:30 in the afternoon four Saturdays in a row, you have put in almost as many hours as you put in the average Sunday school in half a year. It is amazing that we are getting people to do this. This is another effort to show the inter-relationship between the inner city and the suburb.

It is obvious that in anything like this there are dangers. We are working against the tide in that we are emphasizing work with children at this point. My personal feeling is that the children are here now, and we should not ignore them. One of the biggest of the Anti-Poverty Programs is the Get-Set Program which seeks to prevent future dropouts by beginning with children when they are young. I have the hope that maybe we can prevent some dropouts from Christ's church by working with children. I well realize that there must be work with adults, and you must start somewhere, and not all of us are talented at certain kinds of adult work. However, most of us can certainly begin to think in terms of the children, and I still feel that we can reach adults through children.

Another danger is that some of our ministry is addressed to the masses. I don't know how this can be avoided. The masses of the hostile and the ignorant are there. I cannot see hiding our heads in the sand and saying, "Well, we will work with ten people here and twelve people there, and this is all we have to worry about." Certainly in-depth ministry is necessary and important, but as the tide of hostility and ignorance is rushing in, we must think sometimes about how we reach masses as well as how we reach the two's and the three's.

Another obvious danger is that we may be too big. There may be too many congregations involved in our parish. I follow with great interest what is happening in another area where there are seven congregations in a cooperative ministry, or in Camden,

New Jersey, where the Presbyterians have five men in three small congregations. We may be too big and too broad, which could result in shallowness and superficiality. I think that in another year we will know pretty well whether this is going to happen.

This is less an authoritative answer to what it means to be the whole church in the whole community than an effort to share an experiment that is different. In some ways it runs counter to new ideas, and yet it seeks to remove the isolation of congregations, whether they be in suburbia or in the inner city. It also attempts to remove the isolation of special ministries from the regular program of the parish. We are the Body of Christ, and the hand is not to be separated from the foot. It is only when we are together, share each other's ministries, and realize our need to work together that we can be the whole church in the whole community.

Bibliography

Theology

Bertram, Robert W. (ed.), *Theology in the Life of the Church* (Philadelphia: Fortress Press, 1963).

Burtness, James H., and Kildahl, John (ed.), *The New Community in Christ* (Minneapolis: Augsburg, 1963).

Carlson, Edgar M., *The Church and the Public Conscience* (Philadelphia' Fortress Press, 1956).

Danker, William, *Two Worlds or None* (St. Louis: Concordia Publishing House, 1964).

Forell, George W., *Faith Active in Love* (Minneapolis: Augsburg Publishing House, 1962).

Haselden, Kyle, *The Racial Problem in Christian Perspective* (New York: Harper, 1959).

Mays, Benjamin E., *Seeking to Be Christian in Race Relations* (New York: Friendship, 1957).

Newbigin, Lesslie, *Trinitarian Faith and Today's Mission* (Richmond: John Knox Press, 1964).

Pelikan, Jaroslav, *The Light of the World* (New York: Harper and Row, 1962).

Pope, Liston, *The Kingdom Beyond Caste* (New York: Friendship Press, 1957).

Siirala, Aarne, *The Voice of Illness* (Philadelphia: Fortress Press, 1964).

Sittler, Joseph, *The Care of the Earth* (Philadelphia: Fortress Press, 1964).

Vicedom, Georg F., *The Mission of God* (St. Louis: Concordia Publishing House, 1965).

————*Messages of the Helsinki Assembly* (Minneapolis: Augsburg Publishing House).

Renewal of the Church

Barr, Browne, *Parish Back Talk* (New York: Abingdon, 1964).

Bonhoeffer, Dietrich, *Cost of Discipleship* (New York, Harper, 1960).

Bonhoeffer, Dietrich, *Life Together* (New York: Harper, 1954).

Campbell, Will D., *Race and the Renewal of the Church* (Philadelphia: Westminster, 1962).

Fisher, Wallace, *From Tradition to Mission* (Nashville: Abingdon, 1964).

Gibbs and Morton, *God's Frozen People* (Philadelphia: Westminster, 1965).

Greene, Shirley E., *Ferment on the Fringe* (Philadelphia: The Christian Education Press, 1960).

Howe, Ruel, *The Miracle of Dialogue* (New York: Seabury, 1963).

Kloetzli, Walter, *City Church — Death or Renewal* (Philadelphia: Fortress, 1961).

Lehman, Paul, *Ethics in a Christian Context* (New York: Harper and Row, 1963).

Marty, Martin (ed.), *Death and Birth of the Parish* (St. Louis: Concordia, 1964).

Matson, Theodore, *Edge of the Edge* (New York: Friendship Press, 1961).

Raines, Robert, *Reshaping the Christian Life* (New York: Harper and Row, 1964).

Webber, George, *The Congregation in Mission* (Nashville: Abingdon, 1964).

Weber, Hans-Ruedi, *The Militant Ministry* (Philadelphia: Fortress Press, 1963).

———*Salty Christians* (New York, Seabury, 1963).

Wentz, Frederick, *The Laymen's Role Today* (New York: Doubleday, 1963).

Winter, Gibson, *The New Creation as Metropolis* (New York: Macmillan, 1963).

Winter, Gibson, *The Suburban Captivity of the Churches* (New York: Doubleday, 1961).

The Church and the World

Barry, David, *Implications for Mission Policies* (Address given at the Consultation on Community Organization, Division of Home Missions, National Council of Churches, 1964).

Bockelman, Wilfred, *On Good Soil* (New York: Friendship Press, 1959).

Clark, Henry, *The Christian Case Against Poverty* (New York: Association Press, 1965).

Cox, Harvey, *The Secular City* (New York: MacMillan Company, 1965).

Curtis, Charles, "Mission to Vertical Villages," *The City Church,* Volume XV, Number 4, September 1964.

Davies, Alfred T., *The Pulpit Speaks on Race* (Nashville: Abingdon Press, 1956, 1958, 1960, 1963, 1965).

Goodman, Grace, *The Church and the Apartment House* (New York: Division of Church Strategy, Presbyterian Church, 1965).

Gullixson, T. F., *In the Face of the West Wind* (Minneapolis: Augsburg Publishing House, 1963).

Halvorson, Lawrence W., *The Church in a Diverse Society* (Minneapolis: Augsburg Publishing House, 1964).

Hong, Howard, *This World and the Church* (Minneapolis: Augsburg Publishing House, 1955).

Judy, Marvin T., *The Larger Parish and Group Ministry* (Nashville: Abingdon Press, 1957).

Kloetzli, Walter (ed.), *Challenge and Response in the City* (Rock Island: Augustana, 1962).

Kloetzli, Walter, *The Church and the Urban Challenge* (Philadelphia: Fortress Press, 1961).

Kloetzli, Walter and Hillman, Arthur, *Urban Church Planning* (Philadelphia: Fortress Press, 1958).

Lee, Robert (ed.), *The Church and the Exploding Metropolis* (New York: Scribners, 1964).

Leibrecht, Walter, *Being a Christian in Today's World* (Philadelphia: Fortress, 1962).

McBride, C. R., *Protestant Churchmanship for Rural America* (Valley Forge: Judson Press, 1962).

Mueller, E. W. and Ekola, Giles C., *The Silent Struggle for Mid-America* (Minneapolis: Augsburg Publishing House, 1963).

——*Mission in the American Outdoors* (St. Louis: Concordia Publishing House, 1966).

Musselman, Paul, *The Church on the Urban Frontier* (Greenwich: Seabury, 1960).

Norton, Perry L., *Church and Metropolis* (New York: Seabury Press, 1964).

Robinson, John A. T., *On Being the Church in the World* (Philadelphia: Westminster, 1962).

Shippey, Frederick, *Protestantism in Suburban Life* (New York: Abingdon Press, 1964).

Stringfellow, William, *A Private and Public Faith* (Grand Rapids: Eerdman, 1962).

Thielicke, Helmut, *Man in God's World* (New York: Harper and Row, 1963).

Schaller, Lyle, *Urban Renewal and the Church* (Cleveland: Regional Church Planning Office, 1961).

Spike, Robert W., *The Freedom Revolution and the Churches* (New York: Association, 1965).

Williams, Colin, *What in the World* (New York: National Council of Churches, 1964).

——*Where in the World* (New York: National Council of Churches, 1963).

——*The Church and Poverty, American Missions Together* (Chicago: National Lutheran Council, Division of American Missions, July, 1965).

——*Lutheran Witness in a Diverse Society, American Missions Together* (Chicago: National Lutheran Council, Division of American Missions, Jan., 1964).

——*New Thousands in Town and Country* (Chicago: National Lutheran Council, Division of American Missions, 1962).

————*Social Ministry and the Congregation, American Missions To-gether* (Chicago: National Lutheran Council, Division of American Missions, July, 1964).

The Liturgy of the Church

Brown, Edgar S., *Living the Liturgy* (Philadelphia: Fortress Press, 1961).

Dix, Dom Gregory, *The Shape of the Liturgy* (London: Dacre Press, 1945).

Hebert, A. G., *Liturgy and Society* (Naperville, Ill.: Alec Allenson).

Koenker, Ernest B., *Worship in Word and Sacrament* (St. Louis: Concordia Publishing House, 1959).

Lang, P. H. D., *Ceremony and Celebration* (St. Louis: Concordia Publishing House, 1965).

Robinson, John A. T., *On Being the Church in the World* (Philadelphia: Westminster Press, 1960).

Schmenmann, Alexander, *For the Life of the World* (New York: National Student Christian Federation, 1963).

Principles and Suggestions for Liturgical Renewal in Parish Life (Lutheran Society for Worship Music and the Arts, Bulletin No. 18).